# Contents

I0411758

## Tables

## Figure

## Abbreviations

| | |
|---|---|
| CIO | Chief Information Officer |
| DHS | Department of Homeland Security |
| DOD | Department of Defense |
| DOE | Department of Energy |
| FISMA | Federal Information Security Management Act |
| FTC | Federal Trade Commission |
| HUD | Department of Housing and Urban Development |
| NARA | National Archives and Records Administration |
| NASA | National Aeronautics and Space Administration |
| NIST | National Institute of Standards and Technology |
| NRC | Nuclear Regulatory Commission |
| OMB | Office of Management and Budget |
| PIA | privacy impact assessment |
| PII | personally identifiable information |
| SBA | Small Business Administration |
| SSA | Social Security Administration |

**United States Government Accountability Office**
**Washington, DC 20548**

June 28, 2011

Congressional Requesters:

Federal agencies are increasingly using recently developed Internet technologies (commonly referred to as "Web 2.0" technologies) that offer flexible, sophisticated capabilities for interaction with individuals, allowing participants to publish comments, photos, and videos directly on agency-sponsored Web pages. These technologies include services offered by social networking sites (such as Facebook and Twitter) and video-sharing Web sites (such as YouTube), which allow individuals or groups of individuals to create, organize, edit, comment on, and share content.

The use of these services by federal agencies was endorsed in a January 2009 memorandum by President Obama promoting transparency and open government.[1] The memorandum encouraged executive departments and agencies to harness new technologies to put information about their operations and decisions online so that it would be readily available to the public. It also encouraged the solicitation of public feedback to identify information of the greatest use to the public, assess and improve levels of collaboration, and identify new opportunities for cooperation in government. However, while such use of social media offers the potential to better include people in the governing process and further agency missions, use of these services may also pose risks that government records and sensitive information, including personally identifiable information (PII),[2] is not properly managed or protected.

You asked us to review federal agencies' use of commercially provided social media services. Specifically, as agreed with your offices, our objectives were to (1) describe how federal agencies are currently using commercially provided social media services, and (2) determine the extent

---

[1]The White House, *Memorandum for the Heads of Executive Departments and Agencies: Transparency and Open Government* (Washington, D.C.: Jan. 21, 2009).

[2]For purposes of this report, the terms personal information and personally identifiable information are used interchangeably to refer to any information about an individual maintained by an agency, including (1) any information that can be used to distinguish or trace an individual's identity, such as name, Social Security number, date and place of birth, mother's maiden name, or biometric records, and (2) any other information that is linked or linkable to an individual, such as medical, educational, financial, and employment information.

GAO-11-605  Social Media Policies and Procedures

to which federal agencies have developed and implemented policies and procedures for managing and protecting information associated with this use.

To address our first objective, we examined department-level Facebook pages, Twitter accounts, and YouTube channels associated with each of the 24 major federal agencies covered by the Chief Financial Officers Act[3] to describe the types of information agencies disseminated via the services and the nature of their interactions with the public.[4] We categorized agency use based on types of information found on their social media pages.[5] In addition, we interviewed agency officials to discuss the extent to which they collect and use personally identifiable information provided by the public on their social media pages.

To address our second objective, we reviewed pertinent records management, privacy, and security policies, procedures, guidance, and risk assessments in place at each of the 23 major agencies and compared them to relevant federal regulations and guidance on records management, privacy, and security. We also reviewed relevant reports and studies to identify records management, privacy, and security risks associated with social media use by federal agencies. Finally, in coordination with the National Academy of Public Administration,[6] we conducted a roundtable discussion to solicit views on these issues from federal officials involved in agency use of social media.

---

[3]The 24 major departments and agencies are the Departments of Agriculture, Commerce, Defense, Education, Energy, Health and Human Services, Homeland Security, Housing and Urban Development, the Interior, Justice, Labor, State, Transportation, the Treasury, and Veterans Affairs; the Environmental Protection Agency, General Services Administration, National Aeronautics and Space Administration, National Science Foundation, Nuclear Regulatory Commission, Office of Personnel Management, Small Business Administration, Social Security Administration, and U.S. Agency for International Development.

[4]We selected Facebook, Twitter, and YouTube because of their widespread use within the federal government as well as their broad popularity with the public.

[5]Because the Nuclear Regulatory Commission (NRC) did not use Facebook, Twitter, or YouTube at the time of our review, we did not include it as part of our evaluation.

[6]Chartered by Congress in 1967 as an independent, non-partisan organization, the National Academy is a non-profit, independent coalition of public management and organizational leaders that provides insights on key public management issues and advisory services to government agencies.

We conducted this performance audit from July 2010 to June 2011 in accordance with generally accepted government auditing standards. Those standards require that we plan and perform the audit to obtain sufficient, appropriate evidence to provide a reasonable basis for our findings and conclusions based on our audit objectives. We believe that the evidence obtained provides a reasonable basis for our findings and conclusions based on our audit objectives. Our objectives, scope, and methodology are discussed in more detail in appendix I.

## Background

Internet-based services using Web 2.0 technology have become increasingly popular. Web 2.0 technologies are a second generation of the World Wide Web as an enabling platform for Web-based communities of interest, collaboration, and interactive services. These technologies include Web logs (known as "blogs"), which allow individuals to respond online to agency notices and other postings; "wikis," which allow individual users to directly collaborate on the content of Web pages; "podcasting," which allows users to download audio content; and "mashups," which are Web sites that combine content from multiple sources. Web 2.0 technologies also include social media services, which allow individuals or groups of individuals to create, organize, edit, comment on, and share content. These include social networking sites (such as Facebook and Twitter) and video-sharing Web sites (such as YouTube).

While in the past Internet usage concentrated on sites that provide online shopping opportunities and other services, according to the Nielsen Company,[7] social media-related sites have moved to the forefront. In June 2010, it reported that Internet users worldwide accessed social media sites one out of every 4 1/2 minutes they spent online on average. The use of social networking services now reportedly exceeds Web-based e-mail usage, and the number of American users frequenting online video sites has more than tripled since 2003. The Nielsen Company reported that during the month of April 2010, the average user spent nearly 6 hours on social media-related sites.

---

[7]The Nielsen Company is a global information and measurement company in marketing and consumer information, television and other media measurement, online intelligence, mobile measurement, trade shows, and related assets. The company has a presence in approximately 100 countries, with headquarters in New York.

Facebook is a social networking site that lets users create personal profiles describing themselves and then locate and connect with friends, co-workers, and others who share similar interests or who have common backgrounds. Individual profiles may contain—at the user's discretion—detailed personal information, including birth date, home address, telephone number, employment history, educational background, and religious beliefs. Facebook also allows any user to establish a "page" to represent an organization (including federal agencies), business, or public figure in order to disseminate information to users who choose to connect with them. These users can leave comments in response to information posted on such a page. Profile information for these users may be made available to the administrators of these pages, depending on settings controlled by the user. According to the Facebook site, Facebook has over 500 million active users who spend more than 700 billion minutes per month on Facebook.

Twitter is a social networking site that allows users to share and receive information through short messages that are also known as "tweets." These messages are no longer than 140 characters in length. Twitter users can establish accounts by providing a limited amount of PII but may elect to provide additional PII if they wish. Users can post messages to their profile pages and reply to other Twitter users' tweets. Users can "follow" other users as well—i.e., subscribe to their tweets. In March 2011, Twitter reported adding an average of 460,000 new accounts and facilitating the delivery of 140 million tweets every day.

YouTube is a video-sharing site that allows users to discover, watch, upload, comment on, and share originally created videos. Similar to Twitter, users can establish accounts on YouTube with only limited amounts of PII, although they may choose to provide more detailed information on their profile page. Users can comment on videos posted on a page either in written responses or by uploading their own videos.[8] According to YouTube, during 2010 more than 13 million hours of video were uploaded.

Federal agencies are increasingly using these social media tools to enhance services and interactions with the public. As of April 2011, 23 of 24 major federal agencies had established accounts on Facebook, Twitter,

---

[8]An administrator of a YouTube page can elect to remove the ability for users to leave comments.

and YouTube.[9] Furthermore, the public increasingly follows the information provided by federal agencies on these services. For example, as of April 2011, the U.S. Department of State had over 72,000 users following its Facebook page; the National Aeronautics and Space Administration (NASA) had over 992,000 Twitter followers; and a video uploaded by NASA on YouTube in December 2010 had over 360,000 views as of April 2011.

## Federal Agencies Are Responsible for Managing Records, Protecting Privacy, and Ensuring Adequate Security

The Federal Records Act establishes requirements for records management programs in federal agencies. Each federal agency is required to make and preserve records that (1) document the organization, functions, policies, decisions, procedures, and essential transactions of the agency and (2) provide the information necessary to protect the legal and financial rights of the government and of persons directly affected by the agency's activities. The Federal Records Act defines a federal record without respect to format. Records include all books, papers, maps, photographs, machine readable materials, or other documentary materials regardless of physical form or characteristics, made or received by an agency of the government under federal law or in connection with the transaction of public business and preserved or appropriate for preservation by that agency as evidence of the organization, functions, policies, decisions, procedures, operations, or other activities of the government or because of the informational value of data in them.

The agency responsible for providing guidance for adhering to the Federal Records Act is the National Archives and Records Administration (NARA). NARA is responsible for issuing records management guidance; working with agencies to implement effective controls over the creation, maintenance, and use of records in the conduct of agency business; providing oversight of agencies' records management programs; approving the disposition (destruction or preservation) of records; and providing storage facilities for agency records.

In October 2010, NARA issued a bulletin to provide guidance to federal agencies in managing records produced when federal agencies use social media platforms for federal business.[10] The bulletin highlighted the

---

[9]The Nuclear Regulatory Commission (NRC) does not use Facebook, YouTube, or Twitter.

[10]National Archives and Records Administration, Bulletin 2011-02: *Guidance on Managing Records in Web 2.0/Social Media Platforms* (College Park, Md.: Oct. 20, 2010).

requirement for agencies to decide how they will manage records created in social media environments in accordance with applicable federal laws and regulations. As part of this effort, the guidance emphasized the need for active participation of agency records management staff, Web managers, social media managers, information technology staff, privacy and information security staff, and other relevant stakeholders at each federal agency.

## Privacy Laws and Guidance Set Requirements to Ensure the Protection of Personal Information

The primary laws that provide privacy protections for personal information accessed or held by the federal government are the Privacy Act of 1974 and E-Government Act of 2002. These laws describe, among other things, agency responsibilities with regard to protecting PII. The Privacy Act places limitations on agencies' collection, disclosure, and use of personal information maintained in systems of records. A system of records is a collection of information about individuals under control of an agency from which information is retrieved by the name of an individual or other identifier. The E-Government Act of 2002 requires agencies to assess the impact of federal information systems on individuals' privacy. Specifically, the E-Government Act strives to enhance the protection of personal information in government information systems and information collections by requiring agencies to conduct privacy impact assessments (PIA).

A PIA is an analysis of how personal information is collected, stored, shared, and managed in a federal system. Specifically, according to Office of Management and Budget (OMB) guidance, the purpose of a PIA is to (1) ensure handling conforms to applicable legal, regulatory, and policy requirements regarding privacy; (2) determine the risks and effects of collecting, maintaining, and disseminating information in identifiable form in an electronic information system; and (3) examine and evaluate protections and alternative processes for handling information to mitigate potential privacy risks.

In June 2010, OMB issued guidance to federal agencies for protecting privacy when using Web-based technologies (such as social media).[11] The guidance built upon the protections and requirements outlined in the Privacy Act and E-Government Act and called for agencies to develop transparent privacy policies and notices to ensure that agencies provide

---

[11]Office of Management and Budget, Memorandum M-10-23: *Guidance for Agency Use of Third-Party Websites and Applications* (Washington, D.C.: June 25, 2010).

adequate notice of their use of social media services to the public, and to analyze privacy implications whenever federal agencies choose to use such technologies to engage with the public.

## Key Laws and Guidance Set Agencies' Responsibilities for Securing Government Information

The Federal Information Security Management Act of 2002 (FISMA) established a framework designed to ensure the effectiveness of security controls over information resources that support federal operations and assets. According to FISMA, each agency is responsible for, among other things, providing information security protections commensurate with the risk and magnitude of the harm resulting from unauthorized access, use, disclosure, disruption, modification, or destruction of information collected or maintained by or on behalf of the agency and information systems used or operated by an agency or by a contractor of an agency or other organization on behalf of an agency.

Consistent with its statutory responsibilities under FISMA, in August 2009 the National Institute of Standards and Technology (NIST) issued an update to its guidance on recommended security controls for federal information systems and organizations.[12] The NIST guidance directs agencies to select and specify security controls for information systems based on an assessment of the risk to organizational operations and assets, individuals, other organizations, and the nation associated with operation of those systems. According to the guidance, the use of a risk-based approach is applicable not just to the operation of the agency's internal systems but is also important when an agency is using technology for which its ability to establish security controls may be limited, such as when using a third-party social media service.

## GAO Has Identified Challenges in Agencies' Use of Social Media

In July 2010, we testified that while the use of Web 2.0 technologies, including social media technologies, can transform how federal agencies engage the public by allowing citizens to be more involved in the governing process, agency use of such technologies can also present challenges related to records management, privacy, and security.[13]

---

[12]NIST, *Recommended Security Controls for Federal Information Systems and Organizations*, Special Publication 800-53, Revision 3 (Gaithersburg, Md.: August 2009).

[13]GAO, *Information Management: Challenges in Federal Agencies' Use of Web 2.0 Technologies*, GAO-10-872T (Washington, D.C.: July 22, 2010).

GAO-11-605 Social Media Policies and Procedures

- **Records Management:** We reported that Web 2.0 technologies raised issues concerning the government's ability to identify and preserve federal records. Agencies may face challenges in assessing whether the information they generate and receive by means of these technologies constitutes federal records. Furthermore, once the need to preserve information as federal records has been established, mechanisms need to be put in place to capture such records and preserve them properly. We stated that proper records retention management needs to take into account NARA record scheduling requirements and federal law, which require that the disposition of all federal records be planned according to an agency schedule or a general records schedule approved by NARA.

  We highlighted that these requirements may be challenging for agencies because the types of records involved when information is collected via Web 2.0 technologies may not be clear. As previously mentioned, in October 2010, NARA issued further guidance that clarified agency responsibilities in making records determinations.

- **Privacy:** We noted, among other things, that agencies faced challenges in ensuring that they are taking appropriate steps to limit the collection and use of personal information made available through social media. We stated that privacy could be compromised if clear limits were not set on how the government uses personal information to which it has access in social networking environments. Social networking sites, such as Facebook, encourage people to provide personal information that they intend to be used only for social purposes. Government agencies that participate in such sites may have access to this information and may need rules on how such information can be used. While such agencies cannot control what information may be captured by social networking sites, they can make determinations about what information they will collect and what to disclose. However, unless rules to guide their decisions are clear, agencies could handle information inconsistently. OMB's subsequent release of guidance, as previously discussed, clarified agency requirements for such privacy protections.

- **Security:** We highlighted that federal government information systems have been targeted by persistent, pervasive, and aggressive threats and that, as a result, personal and agency information needs to be safeguarded from security threats, and that guidance may be needed for employees on how to use social media Web sites properly and how to handle information in the context of social media.

  Cyber attacks continue to pose a potentially devastating threat to the systems and operations of the federal government. In February 2011, the

Director of National Intelligence testified that, in the previous year, there had been a dramatic increase in malicious cyber activity targeting U.S. computers and networks, including a more than tripling of the volume of malicious software since 2009.[14]

Further, in March 2011, the Federal Trade Commission (FTC) reached an agreement with Twitter to resolve charges that the company deceived consumers and put their privacy at risk by failing to safeguard their personal information. The FTC alleged that serious lapses in the company's security allowed hackers to obtain unauthorized administrative control of Twitter and send unauthorized tweets from user accounts, including one tweet, purportedly from President Obama, that offered his more than 150,000 "followers" a chance to win $500 in free gasoline, in exchange for filling out a survey. To resolve the charges, Twitter agreed to establish and maintain a comprehensive information security program that would be assessed by an independent auditor every other year for 10 years.[15]

According to a Chief Information Officers (CIO) Council report released in September 2009, as the federal government begins to utilize public social media Web sites, advanced persistent threats may be targeted against these Web sites. In addition, attackers may use social media to collect information and launch attacks against federal information systems. Table 1 summarizes three types of security threats identified by the CIO Council that agencies may face when using commercially provided social media services.

---

[14]Director of National Intelligence, Statement for the Record on the Worldwide Threat Assessment of the U.S. Intelligence Community, statement before the Senate Select Committee on Intelligence (Feb. 16, 2011).

[15]Federal Trade Commission, FTC Accepts Final Settlement with Twitter for Failure to Safeguard Personal Information (press release, Mar. 11, 2011), http://www.ftc.gov/opa/2011/03/twitter.shtm.

**Table 1: Examples of Security Threats Agencies Face When Using Commercially Provided Social Media Services**

| Social media threat | Description |
|---|---|
| Spear phishing | An attack targeting a specific user or group of users that attempts to deceive the user into performing an action, such as opening a document or clicking a link, that can lead to a compromise of the user's system by installing malicious software. Spear phishers rely on knowing personal information about their target, such as an event, interest, travel plans, or current issues, that allows them to gain the confidence of their victims. Sometimes this information is gathered by hacking into the targeted network, but often it is easy to look up personal details about target victims on a social media network. |
| Social engineering | An attack using personal information to build trust with a user in order to gain unauthorized access to sensitive information, systems, and networks or to engage in identity fraud, among other things. For example, an attacker may learn personal information about an individual through a social media service and build a trust relationship by expressing interest in similar topics. Once the victim trusts the attacker, the attacker can collect additional information about the user or use their relationship to expand the attacker's influence to other users and friends, further compromising networks and systems and jeopardizing additional individuals. |
| Web application attack | An attack utilizing custom Web applications embedded within social media sites, which can lead to installation of malicious code onto federal computers to be used to gain unauthorized access. A hijacked account of a federal user or a federal account may allow for unauthorized posts, tweets, or messages to be seen by the public as official messages, or may be used to spread malicious software by encouraging users to click links or download unwanted applications. |

Source: GAO analysis of CIO Council data.

The rapid development of social media technologies makes it challenging to keep up with the constantly evolving threats deployed against them and raises the risks associated with government participation in such technologies.

# Federal Agencies Have Used Social Media Services for a Variety of Purposes

Federal agencies have been using social media services to support their individual missions. While Facebook, Twitter, and YouTube offer unique ways for agencies to interact with the public, we identified several distinct ways that federal agencies are using the three social media services. Despite varying features of the three platforms, agency interactions can be broadly categorized by the manner in which information is exchanged with the public, including reposting information already available on an agency Web site, posting original content not available on agency Web sites, soliciting feedback from the public, responding to comments, and linking to non-government Web sites. Figure 1 shows how the 23 agencies[16] use each of these functions.

---

[16]We reviewed agency use of these services from July 2010 through January 2011. Because the Nuclear Regulatory Commission (NRC) did not use any of the three social media services, we did not include it in our evaluation.

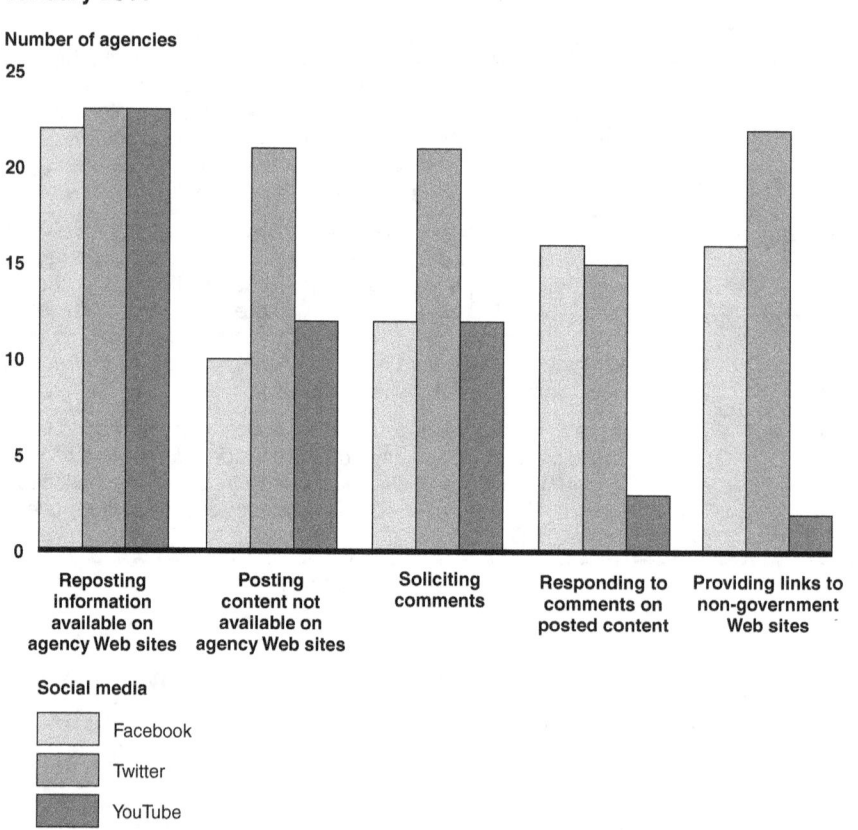

Figure 1: Agency Use of Facebook, Twitter, and YouTube from July 2010 through January 2011

Number of agencies

Social media

- Facebook
- Twitter
- YouTube

Source: GAO analysis of publicly available data.

## Reposting Information Available on Agency Web sites

All 23 agencies used social media to re-post information that is also available on an official agency Web site. This information typically included press releases that agencies issue on mission-related topics or posts to an agency's blog. Each of the three services was used for reposting information by the agencies.

Facebook was used to repost information and direct the public to an agency's official Web site. For example, the Social Security Administration (SSA) posted a notice on its Facebook page that briefly discussed Social Security benefits and provided a link to SSA's Web site. The same information was also posted on the SSA Web page.

Twitter was used to repost information in an abbreviated format, accompanied by a link to an official agency Web page where the full content was available. For example, the Department of the Interior posted a message (or "tweet") about an order that the Secretary of the Interior had issued and provided a link to the agency's Web site where the full order was available.

YouTube was generally used to provide an alternate means of accessing videos that were available on the agencies' Web sites. For example, the Department of Defense (DOD) uploaded a video to its YouTube channel—the Pentagon Channel—that described what was going on at the Pentagon during a particular week. The video was also posted on a DOD Web site dedicated to broadcasting military news and information for members of the armed forces.

## Posting Content Not Available on Agency Web sites

In addition to reposting information, agencies also used social media to post original content that is not available on their Web sites. All 23 agencies used social media to post content not available on the agency's Web site. Twitter was used most often for this purpose.

Facebook was used to post content such as pictures and descriptions of officials on tours or inspections. For example, the Facebook page for the Department of Housing and Urban Development (HUD) featured a picture of the HUD Secretary with President Obama and others while visiting a renovated public housing development during a trip to New Orleans to observe efforts to rebuild the city following Hurricane Katrina. This picture and explanation were not posted to any of HUD's Web sites.

Twitter was often used by agencies to post ephemeral or time-sensitive information. For example, DOD used its Twitter account to encourage its subscribers to sign up to be extras in a movie filming in Washington, D.C. This information and encouragement were not posted on the department's Web site.

YouTube was often used to publish videos of officials discussing topics of interest to the public. An example of this is a video posted to the Department of Energy's (DOE) YouTube channel on August 2, 2010, in which an official discussed a project for a battery-based energy storage system. Neither this video nor a transcript of the video was found on a DOE Web site.

| Soliciting Comments | Agencies also used Facebook, Twitter, and YouTube to request comments from the public. This feedback may be received either through the social media service itself or through an agency Web site. Twenty-two of 23 agencies used social media to solicit comments from the public. Of the 22 agencies soliciting feedback, most used Twitter for this purpose. |
|---|---|

Facebook was generally used for feedback solicitation both when the agency wanted the public to provide comments directly via the social media site and when the agency wanted the public to provide comments through an agency Web site. For example, the Department of Veterans Affairs asked on its Facebook page if the readers liked the redesign of the agency's main Web site. The post received over 50 comments.

Twitter was generally used for feedback solicitation when the agency wanted the public to provide comments through an agency Web site. For example, the Department of Education posted a tweet that requested both teachers and parents to comment on their views of what an effective parent-teacher partnership looks like. The post included a link to the department's blog on its Web site, where individuals could leave comments.

YouTube was also used for feedback solicitation. For example, the Department of Transportation uploaded a video to its YouTube channel asking the public to create and upload videos describing how distracted driving has affected their lives. The video received multiple comments from the public expressing their views on driving and using their cell phones at the same time.

## Responding to Comments on Posted Content

Agencies also used social media to respond to comments from the public that were posted on the agencies social media sites to address both administrative and mission-related topics. In these instances, agency responses to public comments were posted to the same social media Web pages where the original comments appeared. Seventeen of the 23 agencies posted responses to public comments on their social media sites. These agencies generally used Facebook or Twitter the most for this activity, with few agencies responding to comments received on their YouTube channels.

Agencies used Facebook to respond to comments received on their Facebook pages. For example, HUD posted information on its Facebook page regarding the department's allocation of funding for rental assistance for non-elderly persons with disabilities with a link to additional information located on the department's Web site. In response, individuals posted questions and comments, and HUD responded.

Twitter was also used by agencies to respond to comments.[17] For example, a tweet posted by the Small Business Administration (SBA) in response to a comment received from a Twitter user stated that the agency was still tweaking the functionality of a system and as a means to provide better customer service asked what e-mail address the individual used.

## Providing Links to Non-Government Web sites

The agencies we reviewed also used social media sites to post links to non-government Web sites (i.e., a Web site whose address does not end in .gov or is not an agency initiative). For example, agencies often provided links to relevant articles located on news media Web sites. All 23 agencies used social media to post links to non-government Web sites. Of the three social media services, Twitter was used the most, while few agencies used YouTube for this purpose.

Twitter was often used by agencies to post links to Web sites, as many of the tweets that Twitter subscribers receive contain links to Web sites providing further information. For example, the Secretary of Transportation posted a Twitter message about a non-government organization's Web site, along with a link to the site.

---

[17]Twitter differs from the other two social media services in that comments received to a Twitter account are not visible on the account's Twitter page. A tweet in reply to a comment received is indicated by including the "@" symbol and the user name of the original commenter.

# Federal Agencies Have Made Mixed Progress in Developing Policies and Procedures for Managing and Protecting Information Associated with Social Media Use

Federal agencies have made mixed progress in developing records management guidance and assessing privacy and security risks associated with their use of commercially provided social media services. Specifically, 12 of the 23 major federal agencies that use Facebook, Twitter, and YouTube have developed and issued guidance to agency officials that outlines (1) processes and policies for how social media records are identified and managed and (2) record-keeping roles and responsibilities. Further, 12 agencies have updated their privacy policies to describe whether they use personal information made available through social media. In addition, eight agencies conducted privacy impact assessments to identify potential risks associated with agency use of the three services. Finally, seven agencies assessed and documented security risks associated with use of the three services and identified mitigating controls to address those risks. Table 2 outlines the extent to which each of the 23 major federal agencies have developed policies and procedures for use of social media.

| Agency | Records management | Privacy protection | | Security risk management |
|---|---|---|---|---|
| | Document processes and policies and record-keeping roles and responsibilities for how social media records are identified and managed | Update privacy policy to discuss use of PII made available through social media | Conduct privacy impact assessment for social media use | Identify security risks associated with agency use of social media and security controls to mitigate risks |
| Department of Agriculture | ○ | ● | ○ | ● |
| Department of Commerce | ● | ○ | ○ | ○ |
| Department of Defense | ● | ● | ○ | ● |
| Department of Education | ○ | ○ | ◐ | ○ |
| Department of Energy | ● | ● | ● | ○ |
| Department of Health and Human Services | ● | ○ | ○ | ● |
| Department of Homeland Security | ○ | ● | ● | ○ |
| Department of Housing and Urban Development | ● | ● | ● | ○ |
| Department of the Interior | ● | ● | ● | ● |
| Department of Justice | ● | ● | ● | ○ |
| Department of Labor | ● | ○ | ● | ● |
| Department of State | ● | ● | ◐ | ○ |
| Department of Transportation | ● | ○ | ● | ○ |
| Department of the Treasury | ○ | ● | ○ | ○ |
| Department of Veterans Affairs | ○ | ○ | ○ | ● |
| Environmental Protection Agency | ● | ● | ○ | ○ |
| General Services Administration | ● | ○ | ○ | ● |
| National Aeronautics and Space Administration | ○ | ○ | ○ | ○ |
| National Science Foundation | ○ | ● | ● | ○ |
| Office of Personnel Management | ○ | ● | ○ | ○ |
| Small Business Administration | ○ | ○ | ○ | ○ |
| Social Security Administration | ○ | ○ | ○ | ○ |
| U.S. Agency for International Development | ○ | ○ | ○ | ○ |

Source: GAO analysis of agency-provided data.

● - Developed policies and procedures that guided use of Facebook, Twitter and YouTube.
◐ - Developed policies and procedures that guided use of some but not all services.
○ - Did not develop policies and procedures for use of social media services.

## Agencies Have Made Progress in Establishing Guidance for Managing Social Media Records

We previously reported that agencies faced challenges in assessing whether the information they generate and receive by means of these services constitutes federal records and establishing mechanisms for capturing and preserving such records.[18] NARA's October 2010 bulletin on managing social media records highlighted, among other things, the need to ensure that social media policies and procedures articulate clear records management processes and policies and recordkeeping roles and responsibilities. Establishing such guidance can provide a basis for consistently and appropriately categorizing and preserving social media content as records.

Twelve of the 23 major federal agencies have taken steps to include records management guidance in their social media policies and procedures.[19] The scope and breadth of the guidance provided varied with each agency. Specifically, eight of the agencies included general statements directing officials responsible for social media content to conform to agency records management policies in identifying records and how to manage them. For example, the Department of Health and Human Services' social media policy stated that "records management requirements for social media technologies are similar to any other information system and shall be in conformance with existing policy" and provided a Web link to the department's records management policies. Four agencies provided more specific guidance to officials on what social media content constitutes a federal record at their respective agencies. For example, the Department of Justice issued a policy in August 2009 that included a set of questions department officials are to answer in determining the record status of content posted on agency social media pages. Officials were asked to assess, among other things, (a) whether the agency content was original and not published on other agency Web sites, (b) the duration of time the content would need to be retained, and (c) what agency entity would be responsible for preserving and monitoring the information posted on the social media site.

Officials from 10 of the 11 agencies that have not yet documented social media guidance for records management reported taking actions to

---

[18]GAO-10-872T.

[19]The 12 agencies with records management guidance are the Departments of Commerce, Defense, Energy, Health and Human Services, Housing and Urban Development, the Interior, Justice, Labor, State, and Transportation; the Environmental Protection Agency; and the General Services Administration.

develop such guidance.[20] Officials from 1 other agency (the National Science Foundation) stated that they intended to prepare guidance but did not report taking any actions to do so.

However, agency officials are still likely to need clear direction on how to assess social media records when using new technology. NARA noted in a September 2010 study that records management staff in agencies have been overwhelmed by the speed at which agency employees are adopting new social media technologies and that social media adopters have sometimes ignored records management concerns.[21] Until agencies ensure that records management processes and policies and recordkeeping roles and responsibilities are articulated within social media policies, officials responsible for creating and administering content on agency social media sites may not be making appropriate determinations about social media records.

## Agencies Continue to Face Challenges in Establishing Mechanisms for Capturing and Preserving Social Media Records

Once the need to preserve information as federal records has been established, mechanisms need to be put in place to capture such records and preserve them properly. We previously testified that establishing such mechanisms may be challenging for agencies because the types of records involved when information is collected via technologies like social media services may not be clear.[22] Officials at agencies that issued records management guidance for social media generally agreed that determining how to preserve social media content as records remains an issue. For example, officials at the Department of the Interior stated that having information with federal record value on non-government systems—such as those of commercial providers of social media—can create challenges in determining who has control over the information and how and when content should be captured for record-keeping. Participants at a roundtable discussion hosted by the National Academy of Public

---

[20]During the course of our review, 8 agencies reported taking actions to develop records management guidance that were not yet complete: the Departments of Agriculture, Education, Homeland Security, and the Treasury; National Aeronautics and Space Administration; Office of Personnel Management; Small Business Administration, and Social Security Administration. Two additional agencies that had not previously provided information about actions to develop records management guidance did so in comments on a draft of this report. Those agencies included the Department of Veterans Affairs and the U.S. Agency for International Development.

[21]National Archives and Records Administration: *A Report of Federal Web 2.0 Use and Record Value* (Sept. 1, 2010).

[22]GAO-10-872T.

Administration on our behalf also confirmed capturing records as a challenge. One participant suggested that further guidance from NARA to include specific "use cases" as examples would benefit agencies in understanding what approaches can be taken to properly capture and preserve social media records.

NARA recently identified the need for further study of potential mechanisms for capturing social media content as records. In its September 2010 study, NARA noted that an agency may not have sufficient control over its content to apply records management principles due to the nature of a third-party site. Furthermore, social media technology can change quickly with functionality being added or changed that could have an impact on records management. As a result, NARA concluded that it should continue to work with other federal agencies to identify best practices for capturing and managing these records. Within its October 2010 bulletin, NARA presented a list of options for how to preserve social media records, such as Web capture tools to create local versions of sites and convert content to other formats. NARA officials stated that activities are underway to provide further assistance to agencies in determining appropriate methods for capturing social media content as federal records. Specifically, in January 2011 NARA initiated a working group in partnership with the Federal Records Council to evaluate Web 2.0 issues regarding records management and develop strategies for capturing social media content as federal records. However, NARA has yet to establish a time frame for issuing new guidance as a result of these efforts. Until guidance is developed that identifies potential mechanisms for capturing social media content as records, potentially important records of government activity may not be appropriately preserved.

## Agencies Have Made Mixed Progress in Updating Privacy Policies and Assessing Privacy Risks Associated with Use of Social Media Services

Social media services often encourage people to provide extensive personal information that may be accessible to other users of those services. Government agencies that participate in such sites may have access to this information and may need to establish controls on how such information can be used. We previously reported that, while such agencies cannot control what information may be captured by social networking sites, they can make determinations about what information they will collect and how it will be used.[23] In June 2010, OMB issued memorandum M-10-23, which specified a variety of actions agencies should take to

---

[23]GAO-10-872T.

protect individual privacy whenever they use third-party Web sites and applications to engage with the public. Two key requirements established by OMB were the need for each agency to (1) update its privacy policy in order to provide the public with information on whether the agency uses PII made available through its use of third-party Web sites for any purpose, and (2) conduct privacy impact assessments (PIA) whenever an agency's use of a third-party Web site makes PII available to the agency.[24]

Assessing privacy risks is an important element of conducting a PIA because it helps agency officials determine appropriate privacy protection policies and techniques to implement those policies. A privacy risk analysis should be performed to determine the nature of privacy risks and the resulting impact if corrective actions are not implemented to mitigate those risks. Such analysis can be especially helpful in connection with the use of social media because there is a high likelihood that PII will be made available to the agency.

Twelve out of 23 agencies updated their privacy policies to include discussion on the use of personal information made available through social media services.[25] In general, agencies stated that while PII was made available to them through their use of social media services, they did not collect or use the PII. For example, HUD updated the privacy policy on its main Web site, www.hud.gov, to state that "no personally identifiable information (PII) may be requested or collected from [its use of] social media sites." As another example, the Department of Energy included a discussion of its policy of removing PII that may be posted on its social media page, noting that officials reserved the right to moderate or remove comments that include PII.

---

[24]"Making PII available" includes any agency action that causes PII to become available or accessible to the agency, whether or not the agency solicits or collects it.

[25]The 12 agencies with updated privacy policies were the Departments of Agriculture, Defense, Energy, Homeland Security, Housing and Urban Development, the Interior, Justice, State, and the Treasury; the Environmental Protection Agency; the National Science Foundation; and the Office of Personnel Management.

Officials from 5 of the 11 agencies that have not updated their privacy policies reported taking actions to do so.[26] Officials from 6 additional agencies (the Departments of Commerce, Health and Human Services, Labor, and Transportation; the National Aeronautics and Space Administration, and the Social Security Administration) stated that they intended to update their privacy policies but did not report taking any actions to do so.

Eight agencies conducted PIAs to assess the privacy risks associated with their use of the three services.[27] For example, the Department of Homeland Security (DHS) published a PIA that assessed the risks of the agency's use of social networking tools, including the potential for agency access to the personal information of individuals interacting with the department on such sites. To mitigate this risk, the department established a policy of prohibiting the collection of personal information by DHS officials using social media sites. Likewise, the Department of Transportation completed a PIA for the use of third-party Web sites and applications, including Facebook, Twitter, and YouTube. The PIA outlined, among other things, what types of PII may potentially be made available to the agency through its use of social media, including the name, current residence, and age of users who may friend, follow, subscribe to or otherwise interact with an official department page on a third-party site. In these instances, the department's PIA directed officials to avoid capturing and using the PII and to redact any PII contained in screenshots that may be saved for recordkeeping purposes.

Officials from 13 agencies had not completed PIAs for their use of any of the social media services, while an additional 2 agencies performed assessments that only evaluated risks associated with using Facebook. Officials from 10 of these agencies reported taking actions to conduct the

---

[26]During the course of our review, three agencies reported taking actions to initiate updates to their privacy policies although the policies had not yet been changed. These included the Department of Veterans Affairs, Small Business Administration, and U.S. Agency for International Development. Two additional agencies that had not previously provided information about actions to update their privacy policies did so in comments on a draft of this report. Those agencies included the Department of Education and General Services Administration.

[27]Eight agencies completed PIAs that apply to the use of Facebook, Twitter, and YouTube: the Departments of Energy, Homeland Security, Housing and Urban Development, the Interior, Justice, Labor, and Transportation; and the National Science Foundation.

assessments.[28] Officials from 2 other agencies (the Department of State and the Small Business Administration) stated that they intended to conduct assessments but did not report taking any actions to do so. Officials from the other 3 agencies (the Departments of Agriculture and the Treasury; and the General Services Administration) stated that they did not plan to conduct PIAs because they were not planning to collect personal information provided on their social media sites and, therefore, an assessment was unnecessary.

However, OMB's guidance states that when an agency takes action that causes PII to become accessible to agency officials—such as posting information on a Facebook page that allows the public to comment—PIAs are required. Given that agency officials have access to comments that may contain PII and could collect and use the information for another purpose, it is important that an assessment be conducted, even if there are no plans to save the information to an agency system.

Without updating privacy policies and performing and publishing PIAs, agency officials and the public lack assurance that all potential privacy risks have been evaluated and that protections have been identified to mitigate them.

## Agencies Have Made Mixed Progress in Assessing Security Risks Associated with Use of Commercially Provided Social Media Services

Pervasive and sustained cyber attacks continue to pose a potentially devastating threat to the systems and operations of the federal government. As part of managing an effective agencywide information security program to mitigate such threats, FISMA requires that federal agencies conduct periodic assessments of the risk and magnitude of harm that could result from the unauthorized access, use, disclosure, disruption, modification, or destruction of agency information and information systems. To help agencies implement such statutory requirements, NIST developed a risk management framework for agencies to follow in

---

[28]During the course of our review, five agencies reported taking actions to conduct and document PIAs that were not yet complete: the Departments of Commerce, Education, Health and Human Services; Social Security Administration; and U.S. Agency for International Development. Five additional agencies that had not previously provided information about actions to conduct and document PIAs did so in comments on a draft of this report. Those agencies included the Departments of Defense and Veterans Affairs; Environmental Protection Agency; National Aeronautics and Space Administration; and Office of Personnel Management.

developing information security programs.[29] As part of this framework, federal agencies are to assess security risks associated with information systems that process federal agency information and identify security controls that can be used to mitigate the identified risks. In associated guidance, NIST highlighted that using such a risk-based approach is also important in circumstances where an organization is employing information technology beyond its ability to adequately protect essential missions and business functions, such as when using commercially provided social media services.[30] By identifying the potential security threats associated with use of such third-party systems, agencies can establish proper controls and restrictions on agency use.

Seven out of 23 agencies performed and documented security risk assessments concerning their use of the three social media services.[31] For example, the Department of Labor outlined the agency's use of the three tools within one risk assessment, evaluating potential threats and vulnerabilities, and recommended controls to mitigate risks associated with those threats and vulnerabilities. The department identified, among other things, the potential risk of having unauthorized information posted to its social media page by agency officials with social media responsibilities and identified the need for such individuals to receive training on proper use of social media sites. Additionally, a Department of Health and Human Services security document stated that, due to risks associated with use of social media, including the potential for social media sites to be used as a vehicle for transmitting malicious software, the department would block use of social media sites—including Facebook, Twitter, and YouTube—by employees, with specific allowances made for those with documented business needs.

According to officials, 16 agencies had not completed and documented assessments for their use of any of the social media services. Officials from 12 of these agencies reported that they were taking actions to

---

[29]NIST, *Guide for Applying the Risk Management Framework to Federal Information Systems*, Special Publication 800-37, Revision 1 (Gaithersburg, Md.: February 2010).

[30]NIST Special Publication 800-53, Revision 3.

[31]Seven agencies completed security risk assessments for Facebook, Twitter, and YouTube: the Departments of Agriculture, Defense, Health and Human Services, the Interior, Labor, and Veterans Affairs; and the General Services Administration.

GAO-11-605 Social Media Policies and Procedures

conduct security risk assessments but had not yet completed them.[32] Officials from 2 additional agencies (the Department of Commerce and the National Science Foundation) stated that they intended to conduct assessments but did not report taking any actions to do so. Officials at 1 other agency (the Department of State) reported that they did not plan to conduct assessments because their internal policies and procedures did not require them to perform risk assessments. As we previously stated, however, NIST guidance requires the application of the risk management process to social networking uses to establish proper controls and restrictions on agency use. Officials from 1 other agency (the Department of Transportation) reported that they had conducted a security risk assessment but did not document the results. Without such documentation, the agency may lack evidence of the justification and rationale for decisions made based on the risk assessment and, consequently, the assurance that security controls have been implemented to properly address identified security threats.

Without conducting and documenting a risk assessment, agency officials cannot ensure that appropriate controls and mitigation measures are in place to address potentially heightened threats associated with social media, including spear phishing and social engineering.

## Conclusions

Federal agencies are increasingly making use of social media technologies, including Facebook, Twitter, and YouTube, to provide information about agency activities and interact with the public. While the purposes for which agencies use these tools vary, they have the potential to improve the government's ability to disseminate information, interact with the public, and improve services to citizens.

However, the widespread use of social media technologies also introduces risks, and agencies have made mixed progress in establishing appropriate policies and procedures for managing records, protecting the privacy of

---

[32]During the course of our review, 6 agencies reported taking actions to conduct and document security risk assessments that were not yet complete: the Departments of Education, Justice, and the Treasury; Environmental Protection Agency; Small Business Administration; and Social Security Administration. Six additional agencies that had not previously provided information about actions to conduct and document assessments did so in comments on a draft of this report. Those agencies included the Departments of Energy, Homeland Security, and Housing and Urban Development; the National Aeronautical and Space Administration; the Office of Personnel Management; and the U.S. Agency for International Development.

personal information, and ensuring the security of federal systems and information. Specifically, just over half of the major agencies using social media have established policies and procedures for identifying what content generated by social media is necessary to preserve in order to ensure compliance with the Federal Records Act, and they continue to face challenges in effectively capturing social media content as records. Without clear policies and procedures for properly identifying and managing social media records, potentially important records of government activity may not be appropriately preserved. In addition, most agencies have not updated their privacy policies or assessed the impact their use of social media may have on the protection of personal information from improper collection, disclosure, or use, as called for in recent OMB guidance. Performing PIAs and updating privacy policies can provide individuals with better assurance that all potential privacy risks associated with their personal information have been evaluated and that protections have been identified to mitigate them. Finally, most agencies did not have documented assessments of the security risks that social media can pose to federal information or systems in alignment with FISMA requirements, which could result in the loss of sensitive information or unauthorized access to critical systems supporting the operations of the federal government. Without conducting and documenting a risk assessment, agency officials cannot ensure that appropriate controls and mitigation measures are in place to address potentially heightened threats associated with social media, such as spear phishing and social engineering.

# Recommendations for Executive Action

To ensure that federal agencies have adequate guidance to determine the appropriate method for preserving federal records generated by content presented on agency social media sites, we recommend that the Archivist of the United States develop guidance on effectively capturing records from social media sites and that this guidance incorporate best practices.

We are also making 32 recommendations to 21 of the 23 departments and agencies in our review to improve their development and implementation of policies and procedures for managing and protecting information associated with social media use. Appendix II contains these recommendations.

## Agency Comments and Our Evaluation

We sent draft copies of this report to the 23 agencies covered by our review, as well as to the National Archives and Records Administration. We received written or e-mail responses from all the agencies. A summary of their comments and our responses, where appropriate, are provided below.

In providing written comments on a draft of this report, the Archivist of the United States stated that NARA concurred with the recommendation to develop guidance on effectively capturing records from social media sites and that the agency would incorporate best practices in this guidance. NARA's comments are reprinted in appendix III.

Of the 21 agencies to which we made recommendations, 12 (the Departments of Defense, Education, Energy, Homeland Security, Housing and Urban Development, and Veterans Affairs; the Environmental Protection Agency; the National Aeronautics and Space Administration; the National Science Foundation; the Office of Personnel Management; the Social Security Administration; and the U.S. Agency for International Development) agreed with our recommendations.

Two of the 21 agencies (the Departments of Commerce and Health and Human Services) generally agreed with our recommendations but provided qualifying comments:

- In written comments on a draft of the report, the Secretary of Commerce concurred with our two recommendations but provided qualifying comments about the second. Regarding our recommendation that the department conduct and document a security risk assessment to assess security threats associated with agency use of commercially provided social media services and identify security controls that can be used to mitigate the identified threats, he stated that the department had a policy in place that requires risk-based assessments to be conducted of social media technologies used by the department in order to determine if mitigating strategies, such as access or usage limitation, are warranted. However, the department did not provide documentation demonstrating that it had completed and documented any of the required risk assessments. The department's comments are reprinted in appendix IV.

- In an e-mail response on a draft of the report, a Department of Health and Human Services' Senior Information Security Officer stated that the department agreed with our recommendation to update its privacy policy. However, the department disagreed with the perceived finding that it had not made progress in conducting a PIA and reported recent efforts to do so. We did not intend to suggest that the department had not taken any steps to develop a PIA, and we updated our report to clarify that the department has taken actions to develop PIAs for its social media use. However, the agency has not yet completed its PIA and thus may lack assurance that all potential privacy risks have been evaluated and that protections have been identified to mitigate them.

Three of the 21 agencies (the Departments of Agriculture and State; and the General Services Administration) did not concur with all of the recommendations made to them:

• In written comments on a draft of the report, the Department of Agriculture's CIO disagreed with our recommendation that the department conduct and document a privacy impact assessment that evaluates potential privacy risks associated with agency use of social media services and identifies protections to address them. Specifically, the CIO stated that the department had completed a Privacy Threshold Analysis that indicated that a PIA was not required since the department did not solicit, collect, or retain PII through its social media sites. However, as indicated in our report, OMB's guidance states that when an agency takes action that causes PII to become accessible to agency officials—such as posting information on a Facebook page that allows the public to comment—PIAs are required. Without a PIA, the department may lack assurance that all potential privacy risks have been evaluated and that protections have been identified to mitigate them. The Department of Agriculture's comments are reprinted in appendix V.

• In written comments on a draft of the report, the Department of State's Chief Financial Officer concurred with one of our two recommendations, but not the other. Specifically, regarding our recommendation that the department conduct and document a security risk assessment to assess security threats associated with agency use of commercially provided social media services and identify security controls that can be used to mitigate the identified threats, he stated that the department shared GAO's concern regarding the security of information in commercially provided social media but that since the department had already determined that its use of social media sites would be limited to providing the public with "low-impact" information, no further risk assessment or certification and accreditation was required. He further stated that the impact on confidentiality, integrity, and availability of systems with such non-structured data could only be determined by policy, not by risk analysis and, therefore, a security risk assessment was not warranted. However, although limiting the type of information that is processed on third-party systems can be an effective mitigating security control, without conducting and documenting a risk assessment, agency officials cannot ensure that policies and mitigation measures effectively address potentially heightened threats associated with social media, including spear phishing and social engineering. The Department of State's comments are reprinted in appendix VI.

- In written comments on a draft of the report, the Administrator of the General Services Administration partially agreed with our two recommendations. Regarding our recommendation that the agency update its privacy policies to describe whether PII made available through its use of social media services is collected and used, the Administrator noted that the agency was updating its privacy directive to describe the agency's practices for handling PII made available through the use of social media. Accordingly, we have updated our report to indicate that the agency has taken actions to update its privacy policies for its use of social media. Regarding our recommendation that the agency conduct and document a privacy impact assessment that evaluates potential privacy risks associated with agency use of social media services and identifies protections to address them, the Administrator stated that no PII is sought by or provided to GSA as a result of the agency's use of Facebook, YouTube, and Twitter and, therefore, the agency determined that conducting a PIA was unnecessary. However, as indicated in our report, OMB's guidance states that when an agency takes action that causes PII to become accessible to agency officials—such as posting information on a Facebook page that allows the public to comment—PIAs are required. Without a PIA, the department may lack assurance that all potential privacy risks have been evaluated and that protections have been identified to mitigate them. The General Services Administration's comments are reprinted in appendix VII.

Four of the 21 agencies did not comment on the recommendations addressed to them. Specifically, the Departments of Labor and Transportation reported that they did not have any comments and the Department of the Treasury and Small Business Administration only provided technical comments, which we addressed in the final report as appropriate.

In cases where these 21 agencies also provided technical comments, we have addressed them in the final report as appropriate. Agencies also provided with their comments information regarding actions completed or underway to address our findings and recommendations and we updated our report to recognize those efforts.[33] Additional written comments are reprinted in appendices VIII through XVII.

We also received e-mail responses from the 2 agencies to which we did not make recommendations. Specifically, the Department of the Interior provided technical comments via e-mail and the Department of Justice stated that it did not have comments on the draft of this report.

As agreed with your office, unless you publicly announce the contents of this report earlier, we plan no further distribution until 30 days from the report date. We will then send copies of this report to other interested congressional committees, Secretaries of the Departments of Agriculture, Commerce, Defense, Education, Energy, Health and Human Services, Homeland Security, Housing and Urban Development, the Interior, Labor, State, Transportation, the Treasury, and Veterans Affairs; the Attorney General; the Administrators of the Environmental Protection Agency, General Services Administration, National Aeronautics and Space Administration, Small Business Administration, and U.S. Agency for International Development; the Commissioner of the Social Security Administration; the Directors of the National Science Foundation and Office of Personnel Management; and the Archivist of the United States. The report will also be available at no charge on the GAO Web site at http://www.gao.gov.

---

[33] The agencies that included information on actions taken to address requirements within comments on a draft of this report were the Departments of Agriculture, Defense, Education, Energy, Homeland Security, Housing and Urban Development, State, the Treasury, and Veterans Affairs; the Environmental Protection Agency; the General Services Administration; the National Aeronautics and Space Administration; the Office of Personnel Management; the Small Business Administration; and the U.S. Agency for International Development.

If you or your staff have any questions regarding this report, please contact me at (202) 512-6244 or at wilshuseng@gao.gov. Contact points for our Offices of Congressional Relations and Public Affairs may be found on the last page of this report. Key contributors to this report are listed in appendix XVIII.

Gregory C. Wilshusen
Director, Information Security Issues

*List of Requesters*

The Honorable Joseph I. Lieberman
Chairman
Committee on Homeland Security
  and Governmental Affairs
United States Senate

The Honorable Thomas R. Carper
Chairman
Subcommittee on Federal Financial Management,
  Government Information, Federal Services,
  and International Security
Committee on Homeland Security
  and Governmental Affairs
United States Senate

The Honorable Mark L. Pryor
Chairman
Subcommittee on Disaster Recovery
  and Intergovernmental Affairs
Committee on Homeland Security
  and Governmental Affairs
United States Senate

The Honorable Elijah Cummings
Ranking Member
Committee on Oversight and Government Reform
House of Representatives

The Honorable Wm. Lacy Clay
House of Representatives

# Appendix I: Objectives, Scope, and Methodology

Our objectives were to:

- describe how agencies are currently using commercially provided social media services, and

- determine the extent to which federal agencies have developed and implemented policies and procedures for managing and protecting information associated with the use of commercially provided social media services.

To address our first objective, we examined the headquarters-level Facebook pages, Twitter accounts, and YouTube channels associated with each of the 24 major federal agencies covered by the Chief Financial Officers Act[1] to describe the types of information agencies disseminated via the services and the nature of their interactions with the public.[2] We selected these three services because of their widespread use within the federal government (23 out of 24 major agencies use each of the services) as well as their broad popularity with the public. We reviewed content on the social media pages, including agency posts as well as comments provided by the public, from July 2010 through January 2011. We categorized agency use based on types of information found on their social media pages. These categories were (1) reposting information available on agency Web sites; (2) posting content not available on agency Web sites; (3) soliciting comments; (4) responding to comments on posted content; and (5) providing links to non-government Web sites. Each agency social media page was reviewed by an analyst to determine whether information had been posted that fell into one of the five categories. Each identified example was corroborated by a second analyst. In the event no examples were identified for an agency in a specific category by the first analyst, the second analyst conducted an additional independent review of agency posts to confirm that none existed.

---

[1]The 24 major departments and agencies are the Departments of Agriculture, Commerce, Defense, Education, Energy, Health and Human Services, Homeland Security, Housing and Urban Development, the Interior, Justice, Labor, State, Transportation, the Treasury, and Veterans Affairs; the Environmental Protection Agency, General Services Administration, National Aeronautics and Space Administration, National Science Foundation, Nuclear Regulatory Commission, Office of Personnel Management, Small Business Administration, Social Security Administration, and U.S. Agency for International Development.

[2]At the time of our review, the Nuclear Regulatory Commission (NRC) did not use Facebook, Twitter, or YouTube. Additionally, the Department of Health and Human Services did not maintain a Facebook page to represent its headquarters, although various components of HHS maintained their own Facebook pages.

To address our second objective, we reviewed pertinent records
management, privacy, and security policies, procedures, guidance, and
risk assessments in place at each of the 23 federal agencies and compared
them to relevant federal records management, privacy, and security laws,
regulations, and guidance.[3] These included the Federal Records Act, the
Privacy Act of 1974, the E-Government Act of 2002, the Federal
Information Security Management Act of 2002 (FISMA), as well as
guidance from the National Archives and Records Administration (NARA),
Office of Management and Budget (OMB), and National Institute of
Standards and Technology (NIST). We interviewed officials at each of
these agencies to discuss recent efforts to oversee the development of
social media policies and procedures and assess risks. We also reviewed
relevant reports and studies to identify records management, privacy, and
security risks associated with social media use by federal agencies. We
interviewed officials from OMB, NARA, and NIST, and members of the
Chief Information Officer Council to develop further understanding of
federal agency requirements for properly managing and protecting
information associated with social media use. Further, we coordinated
with the National Academy of Public Administration, which hosted a
roundtable discussion on our behalf where views on these issues were
solicited from federal agency officials involved in agency use of social
media. Finally, we interviewed representatives of Facebook, Twitter, and
YouTube to discuss records management, privacy, and security issues and
their current and planned approaches regarding interactions with federal
agencies.

We conducted this performance audit from July 2010 to June 2011 in the
Washington, D.C., area, in accordance with generally accepted government
auditing standards. Those standards require that we plan and perform the
audit to obtain sufficient, appropriate evidence to provide a reasonable
basis for our findings and conclusions based on our audit objectives. We
believe that the evidence obtained provides a reasonable basis for our
findings and conclusions based on our audit objectives.

---

[3]Because NRC did not use Facebook, Twitter, or YouTube at the time of our review, we did
not include it in our evaluation of social media policies and procedures.

# Appendix II: Recommendations to Departments and Agencies

| | |
|---|---|
| **Department of Agriculture** | To ensure that appropriate privacy measures are in place when commercially provided social media services are used, we recommend that the Secretary of Agriculture take the following action:<br><br>• Conduct and document a privacy impact assessment that evaluates potential privacy risks associated with agency use of social media services and identifies protections to address them. |
| **Department of Commerce** | To ensure that appropriate privacy and security measures are in place when commercially provided social media services are used, we recommend that the Secretary of Commerce take the following two actions:<br><br>• Update privacy policies to describe whether PII made available through use of social media services is collected and used.<br><br>• Conduct and document a security risk assessment to assess security threats associated with agency use of commercially provided social media services and identify security controls that can be used to mitigate the identified threats. |
| **Department of Defense** | To ensure that appropriate privacy and security measures are in place when commercially provided social media services are used, we recommend that the Secretary of Defense take the following action:<br><br>• Conduct and document a privacy impact assessment that evaluates potential privacy risks associated with agency use of social media services and identifies protections to address them. |
| **Department of Education** | To ensure that appropriate privacy measures are in place when commercially provided social media services are used, we recommend that the Secretary of Education take the following action:<br><br>• Update privacy policies to describe whether PII made available through use of social media services is collected and used. |
| **Department of Energy** | To ensure that appropriate security measures are in place when commercially provided social media services are used, we recommend that the Secretary of Energy take the following action: |

- Conduct and document a security risk assessment to assess security threats associated with agency use of commercially provided social media services and identify security controls that can be used to mitigate the identified threats.

## Department of Health and Human Services

To ensure that appropriate privacy measures are in place when commercially provided social media services are used, we recommend that the Secretary of Health and Human Services take the following action:

- Update privacy policies to describe whether PII made available through use of social media services is collected and used.

## Department of Homeland Security

To ensure that appropriate security measures are in place when commercially provided social media services are used, we recommend that the Secretary of Homeland Security take the following action:

- Conduct and document a security risk assessment to assess security threats associated with agency use of commercially provided social media services and identify security controls that can be used to mitigate the identified threats.

## Department of Housing and Urban Development

To ensure that appropriate security measures are in place when commercially provided social media services are used, we recommend that the Secretary of Housing and Urban Development take the following action:

- Conduct and document a security risk assessment to assess security threats associated with agency use of Twitter and YouTube and identify security controls that can be used to mitigate the identified threats.

## Department of Labor

To ensure that appropriate privacy measures are in place when commercially provided social media services are used, we recommend that the Secretary of Labor take the following action:

- Update privacy policies to describe whether PII made available through use of social media services is collected and used.

| | |
|---|---|
| **Department of State** | To ensure that appropriate privacy and security measures are in place when commercially provided social media services are used, we recommend that the Secretary of State take the following two actions: |

- Conduct and document a privacy impact assessment that evaluates potential privacy risks associated with agency use of Twitter and YouTube and identifies protections to address them.

- Conduct and document a security risk assessment to assess security threats associated with agency use of commercially provided social media services and identify security controls that can be used to mitigate the identified threats.

| | |
|---|---|
| **Department of Transportation** | To ensure that appropriate privacy and security measures are in place when commercially provided social media services are used, we recommend that the Secretary of Transportation take the following two actions: |

- Update privacy policies to describe whether PII made available through use of social media services is collected and used.

- Conduct and document a security risk assessment to assess security threats associated with agency use of commercially provided social media services and identify security controls that can be used to mitigate the identified threats.

| | |
|---|---|
| **Department of the Treasury** | To ensure that appropriate privacy measures are in place when commercially provided social media services are used, we recommend that the Secretary of the Treasury take the following action: |

- Conduct and document a privacy impact assessment that evaluates potential privacy risks associated with agency use of social media services and identifies protections to address them.

| | |
|---|---|
| **Department of Veterans Affairs** | To ensure that appropriate records management and privacy measures are in place when commercially provided social media services are used, we recommend that the Secretary of Veterans Affairs take the following two actions: |

- Add records management guidance to agency social media policies that describes records management processes and policies and recordkeeping roles and responsibilities.

- Conduct and document a privacy impact assessment that evaluates potential privacy risks associated with agency use of social media services and identifies protections to address them.

| Environmental Protection Agency | To ensure that appropriate privacy and security measures are in place when commercially provided social media services are used, we recommend that the Administrator of the Environmental Protection Agency take the following two actions: |
|---|---|

- Conduct and document a privacy impact assessment that evaluates potential privacy risks associated with agency use of social media services and identifies protections to address them.

- Conduct and document a security risk assessment to assess security threats associated with agency use of commercially provided social media services and identify security controls that can be used to mitigate the identified threats.

| General Services Administration | To ensure that appropriate privacy measures are in place when commercially provided social media services are used, we recommend that the Administrator of the General Services Administration take the following two actions: |
|---|---|

- Update privacy policies to describe whether PII made available through use of social media services is collected and used.

- Conduct and document a privacy impact assessment that evaluates potential privacy risks associated with agency use of social media services and identifies protections to address them.

| National Aeronautics and Space Administration | To ensure that appropriate privacy and security measures are in place when commercially provided social media services are used, we recommend that the Administrator of the National Aeronautics and Space Administration take the following three actions: |
|---|---|

- Update privacy policies to describe whether PII made available through use of social media services is collected and used.

- Conduct and document a privacy impact assessment that evaluates potential privacy risks associated with agency use of social media services and identifies protections to address them.

- Conduct and document a security risk assessment to assess security threats associated with agency use of commercially provided social media services and identify security controls that can be used to mitigate the identified threats.

## National Science Foundation

To ensure that appropriate records management and security measures are in place when commercially provided social media services are used, we recommend that the Director of the National Science Foundation take the following two actions:

- Add records management guidance to agency social media policies that describes records management processes and policies and recordkeeping roles and responsibilities.

- Conduct and document a security risk assessment to assess security threats associated with agency use of commercially provided social media services and identify security controls that can be used to mitigate the identified threats.

## Office of Personnel Management

To ensure that appropriate privacy and security measures are in place when commercially provided social media services are used, we recommend that the Director of the Office of Personnel Management take the following two actions:

- Conduct and document a privacy impact assessment that evaluates potential privacy risks associated with agency use of social media services and identifies protections to address them.

- Conduct and document a security risk assessment to assess security threats associated with agency use of commercially provided social media services and identify security controls that can be used to mitigate the identified threats.

## Small Business Administration

To ensure that appropriate privacy measures are in place when commercially provided social media services are used, we recommend that the Administrator of the Small Business Administration take the following action:

- Conduct and document a privacy impact assessment that evaluates potential privacy risks associated with agency use of social media services and identifies protections to address them.

## Social Security Administration

To ensure that appropriate privacy measures are in place when commercially provided social media services are used, we recommend that the Commissioner of the Social Security Administration take the following action:

- Update privacy policies to describe whether PII made available through use of social media services is collected and used.

## U.S. Agency for International Development

To ensure that appropriate records management and security measures are in place when commercially provided social media services are used, we recommend that the Administrator of the U.S. Agency for International Development take the following two actions:

- Add records management guidance to agency social media policies that describes records management processes and policies and recordkeeping roles and responsibilities.

- Conduct and document a security risk assessment to assess security threats associated with agency use of commercially provided social media services and identify security controls that can be used to mitigate the identified threats.

Via email

MAY 2 4 2011

Gregory C. Wilshusen
Director, Information Security Issues
United States Government Accountability Office
44 G Street, NW
Washington, DC 20548

Dear Mr. Wilshusen,

Thank you for the opportunity to review and comment on the draft report GAO-11-605, *SOCIAL MEDIA: Federal Agencies Need Policies and Procedures for Managing and Protecting Information They Access and Disseminate.* We are pleased to note the positive recognition of our October 2010 bulletin on managing social media records as a basis for consistently and appropriately categorizing and preserving social media content as records.

We concur with the recommendation that NARA develop guidance on effectively capturing records from social media sites, and will incorporate best practices in this guidance.

If you have questions regarding this information, please contact Mary Drak by email at mary.drak@nara.gov or by phone at 301-837-1668.

David S. Ferriero
Archivist of the United States

NATIONAL ARCHIVES *and*
RECORDS ADMINISTRATION
8601 ADELPHI ROAD
COLLEGE PARK, MD 20740-6001
*www.archives.gov*

# Appendix IV: Comments from the Department of Commerce

Note: GAO's comments supplementing those in the report's text appear at the end of this appendix.

May 27, 2011

Mr. Gregory C. Wilshusen
Director, Information Security Issues
U.S. Government Accountability Office
Washington, DC 20548

Dear Mr. Wilshusen:

Thank you for the opportunity to comment on the draft report from the U.S. Government Accountability Office (GAO) entitled, *Social Media: Federal Agencies Need Policies and Procedures for Managing and Protecting Information They Access and Disseminate* (GAO-11-605). The Department of Commerce (Department) takes very seriously the privacy of visitors to all its Web sites, including its social media presence.

We concur with the report's recommendation that the Department should update its privacy policies to reflect in more detail the importance of addressing personally identifiable information when employing social media. We do note that the Department of Commerce Policy on the Approval and Use of Social Media and Web 2.0 does stipulate that privacy impact assessments must be addressed and privacy policy statements must be formulated when establishing a social media site.

See comment 1.

Regarding the second GAO recommendation, we concur with the important emphasis on conducting security risk assessments and identifying security controls to mitigate risks associated with agency use of social media services. The Department's Policy on the Approval and Use of Social Media and Web 2.0 requires bureau Chief Information Officers to carry out a risk-based assessment of social media technologies, in accordance with National Institute of Standards and Technology and the Federal Information Security Management Act (FISMA) IT security risk management framework principles, before such technologies are put into use. The policy requires this assessment to address whether access to that technology should be permitted, and whether any limitations on access or usage, e.g., to potentially include IT security controls, are warranted. The policy also dedicates a section to security guidelines and recommends a variety of mitigating controls that touch on various families of FISMA controls, including account administration, password control, password requirements, permission levels, desktop computer and browser configuration, scanning of files, and account monitoring.

Mr. Gregory C. Wilshusen
Page 2

We believe that the risk assessments required by the Department's policy effectively meet the spirit of the GAO recommendation. If the GAO recommendation is meant to imply that a single high-level risk assessment of the use of social media services should be conducted, we believe that such an assessment would not capture the local context of each individual use of social media services. Risk assessments of each instance of social media use include the particular use case, specifics regarding the information involved, purpose of, and mission need supported by the use of such services. We feel that conducting a risk assessment for each use, as required by the Department's policy, better captures details regarding the usage, and consequently, more clearly elucidates the risks and risk-related tradeoffs than carrying out a single assessment.

We are currently in the process of revising our privacy policy to address that recommendation and look forward to receiving the final report. If you have any questions regarding the Department's response, please contact Diana Hynek in the Office of the Chief Information Officer at (202) 482-0266.

Sincerely,

Gary Locke

The following are GAO's comments to the U.S. Department of Commerce's
letter dated May 27, 2011.

## GAO Comments

1. The department did not provide documentation demonstrating that it
   had completed and documented any of the required risk assessments.

# Appendix V: Comments from the U.S. Department of Agriculture

Note: GAO's comments supplementing those in the report's text appear at the end of this appendix.

United States
Department of
Agriculture

MAY 2 / 2011

Office of the Chief
Information Officer

1400 Independence
Avenue S.W.

Washington, DC
20250

TO:     Gregory Wilshusen
        Director, Information Security Issues
        Government Accountability Office

FROM:   Christopher L. Smith
        Chief Information Officer
        Office of the Chief Information Officer

SUBJECT:  U. S. Department of Agriculture Review of GAO Draft Report
          GAO-11-605 "Social Media – Federal Agencies Need Policies and
          Procedures for Managing and Protecting Information They Access and
          Disseminate"

Thank you for the opportunity to review the subject Draft Report. In response to
GAO's findings, conclusions, and recommendations, the U.S. Department of
Agriculture (USDA) submits the following responses:

Table 2: Extent to Which Major Federal Agencies Have Developed Policies and
Procedures for Using Social Media
1. Document processes and policies and record-keeping roles and
   responsibilities for how social media records are identified and managed.
   a. USDA partially agrees with this finding. USDA provided the
      following information in writing to GAO on this issue during this
      social media use engagement:
      i. The records management policy addresses identifying and
         managing records in all media, regardless of physical form
         or characteristics (paper and electronic including email and
         web sites) throughout their life cycle. USDA policy
         documentation relating to records management can be
         found in attachment A, Departmental Regulation
         DR 3080-001 "Records Management."
      ii. We are awaiting guidance from the National Archives and
          Records Administration (NARA) that will specifically
          address strategies for capturing, preserving and managing
          social media electronic records throughout their life cycle.
          We will update USDA policies accordingly once NARA
          guidance becomes available.
      iii. USDA maintains records of comments on the blog, takes
           screen shots of deleted comments on Facebook, and saves
           text from Facebook chats. The Office of Communications
           is currently evaluating Twitter archiving tools available in
           the market place.

See comment 1.

iv. USDA is currently in the process of drafting a social media record keeping System of Records Notice.

Since the completion of GAO's engagement at USDA, the Department has completed its draft policy titled "New Media Roles, Responsibilities and Authorities" (attachment B). This draft policy addresses records management across all aspects of Web 2.0 media. This draft policy is currently under internal USDA review.

2. Update Privacy policy to discuss use of Personally Identifiable Information (PII) made available through social media.

    a. <u>USDA partially agrees with this finding</u>. USDA has updated their Privacy Policy Statement on its social media web site to specifically address Privacy Act protected data. Please see screen shot from USDA's Social Media and Tools web page (attachment C).

See comment 2.

    b. Additionally, USDA has updated its Privacy Policy, draft Departmental Regulation 3515-XXX (attachment D) to address the collection of PII via USDA web sites:

> "Every USDA Web site must clearly and concisely inform visitors about what information the Web site collects about individuals, why the information is collected, and how it is used. No agency/mission area will collect personal information about individuals when they visit USDA Web sites unless the visitor chooses to provide that information"

See comment 3.

3. Conduct Privacy Impact Assessment (PIA) for social media use.

    a. <u>USDA disagrees with this finding</u>. USDA completed a Privacy Threshold Analysis (PTA) on the use of social media by USDA on September 14, 2010 (attachment E). The results of this PTA indicate that a PIA is not required for social media use within USDA.

GAO recommendation to USDA:

Conduct and document a PIA that evaluates potential privacy risks associated with agency use of social media services and identifies protections to address them.

USDA Response:

USDA completed a PTA on the use of social media as a public communications vehicle on September 14, 2010. The results of the PTA indicated that a PIA was not required as USDA does not solicit, collect or retain PII through its social media sites.

USDA uses social media to increase its public information outreach programs beyond USDA.gov internet web presence. USDA does not solicit nor collect PII from the public via its social media presence. Please see the attachment E,

2

USDA Privacy Threshold Analysis (Social Media Websites (Facebook, Twitter, and YouTube).

If further information is needed, please contact Sherry Linkins, Office of the Chief Information Officer Audit Liaison, at 202-720-9293.

Attachments

cc: Richard Coffee, Acting ACIO-CPPO
    Yvonne Jackson, ACIO-TPA&E
    Christopher Lowe, ACIO-ASOC
    Ravoyne Payton, USDA Privacy Officer
    Cynthia Schwind, OCIO
    Sherry Linkins, Audit Liaison, OCIO
    Wayne Moore, Director Office of Communications
    Lennetta Elias, Program Analyst, OCFO

3

The following are GAO's comments to the U.S. Department of Agriculture's letter dated May 27, 2011.

## GAO Comments

1. After reviewing additional documentation and comments provided by department representatives, we updated our report to indicate that the department asserted that it is taking actions to develop records management guidance for social media use, although it has not yet been completed. We have not evaluated these actions.

2. After reviewing the updated privacy policy on the Department's Web site, we agree that the agency has met the requirement, and we have modified table 2 in the final report to reflect that the department has updated its policy.

3. We believe that a PIA is required. As indicated in our report, OMB's guidance states that when an agency takes action that causes PII to become accessible to agency officials—such as posting information on a Facebook page that allows the public to comment—PIAs are required. Without a PIA, the department may lack assurance that all potential privacy risks have been evaluated and that protections have been identified to mitigate them.

# Appendix VI: Comments from the Department of State

Note: GAO's comments supplementing those in the report's text appear at the end of this appendix.

Ms. Jacquelyn Williams-Bridgers
Managing Director
International Affairs and Trade
Government Accountability Office
441 G Street, N.W.
Washington, D.C. 20548-0001

MAY 3 1 2011

Dear Ms. Williams-Bridgers:

We appreciate the opportunity to review your draft report, "SOCIAL MEDIA: Federal Agencies Need Policies and Procedures for Managing and Protecting Information They Access and Disseminate," GAO Job Code 311048.

The enclosed Department of State comments are provided for incorporation with this letter as an appendix to the final report.

If you have any questions concerning this response, please contact Christina Jones, Privacy Division Chief, Bureau of Administration at (202) 261-8407 and George Moore, Chief Computer Scientist, Bureau of Information Resource Management at (703) 812-2203.

Sincerely,

James L. Millette

cc: GAO – Greg Wilshusen
A – William H. Moser
IRM – Susan H. Swart
State/OIG – Evelyn Klemstine

**Department of State Comments on GAO Draft Report**

**SOCIAL MEDIA: Federal Agencies Need Policies and Procedures for
Managing and Protecting Information They Access and Disseminate**
(GAO-11-6050 GAO Code 311048)

The Department of State appreciates the opportunity to comment on GAO's draft
report, *"SOCIAL MEDIA: Federal Agencies Need Policies and Procedures for
Managing and Protecting Information They Access and Disseminate."*

**Recommendation:** Conduct and document a privacy impact assessment that
evaluates potential privacy risks associated with agency use of Twitter and
YouTube and identifies protections to address them.

See comment 1.

**Response:** The Department concurs with the recommendation and has reviewed
its current policy on privacy impact assessments (PIA). To that end, the
Department will revise the current Facebook PIA to reflect a more comprehensive
risk assessment that will incorporate all social media technologies, such as
YouTube and Twitter.

**Recommendation:** Conduct and document a security risk assessment to assess
security threats associated with agency use of commercially provided social media
services and identify security controls that can be used to mitigate the identified
threats.

See comment 2.

**Response:** The Department shares GAO's concern regarding the security of
information in commercially provided social media. However, the Department
disagrees with the GAO recommendation, as stated.

The State Internet Steering Committee recently developed a policy for State
officials who use such sites in an official capacity. This policy is being
incorporated into training modules and user agreements to ensure that these
officials keep sensitive information off of these sites. The Department has already
determined that use of social media sites to provide communication with the public
is a valuable tool so long as only low-impact information is provided. Moreover,
as long as this policy is followed, no further risk assessment and/or certification
and accreditation is required.

2

Note that no a-priori risk assessment of these sites is likely to provide meaningful results, since the data is non-structured, and uninformed users could (if careless or malicious) place sensitive information on these sites, just as they could currently leak it to the press. The impact on confidentiality, integrity, and availability of systems with such non-structured data can only be determined by policy (limit data to low-impact data, for example), not by risk analysis. Therefore, in our view a Security Risk Assessment at State is not warranted at this time.

The following are GAO's comments to the Department of State's letter
dated May 31, 2011.

## GAO Comments

1. After reviewing additional comments provided by department
representatives, we updated our report to indicate that the department
has plans to develop a PIA for its use of YouTube and Twitter.

2. We believe that conducting and documenting a risk assessment is
necessary. Although limiting the type of information that is processed
on third-party systems can be an effective mitigating security control,
without conducting and documenting a risk assessment, agency
officials cannot ensure that appropriate controls and mitigation
measures are in place to address potentially heightened threats
associated with social media, including spear phishing and social
engineering.

Note: GAO's comments
supplementing those in
the report's text appear at
the end of this appendix.

The Honorable Gene L. Dodaro
Comptroller General of the United States
U.S. Government Accountability Office
Washington, DC 20548

Dear Mr. Dodaro:

The U.S. General Services Administration (GSA) appreciates the opportunity to review
and comment on the draft report, "Social Media: Federal Agencies Need Policies and
Procedures for Managing and Protecting Information They Access and Disseminate"
(GAO-11-605). The U.S. Government Accountability Office (GAO) recommends that
the GSA Administrator ensure that appropriate privacy measures are in place when
commercially provided social media services are used. GAO recommended two
specific actions for GSA, discussed below. We agree in part to both recommendations.
GSA is in the process of updating our privacy policy and provides clarifying information
regarding GSA's use of Privacy Impact Assessments (PIA's).

<u>Recommendation 1</u>: GAO recommends GSA "[u]pdate privacy policies to describe
whether PII made available through use of social media services is collected and used."

GSA takes its responsibilities regarding the protection of individuals' PII seriously. For
example, GSA's new Social Media Navigator, available at www.gsa.gov/socialmedia,
states the Agency's privacy policy relative to social media. It contains:

> Privacy Considerations: The Government requires public-facing websites to conduct privacy impact
> assessments if they collect personally identifiable information. They should post a "Privacy Act
> Statement" that describes the Agency's legal authority for collecting personal data and how the data will
> be used. Privacy policies on each website are also required in a standardized machine-readable format
> such as the Platform for Privacy Preferences Project, or P3P. Information on Web 2.0 platforms is
> accessible by others, so do not disclose Privacy Act protected information or other personally
> identifiable information unless authorized to do so in that medium.

See comment 1.

Furthermore, since our initial meetings with GAO, the Privacy Office studied other
agencies' privacy policies that incorporate guidance relative to social media.
Accordingly, GSA is updating its Privacy Directive to state the Agency's practice of
handling PII when it is made available through the use of social media. The revised
directive will be posted when it has completed the concurrence process.

<u>Recommendation 2</u>: GAO recommends GSA "[c]onduct and document a privacy impact
assessment that evaluates potential privacy risks associated with agency use of social
media services and identifies protections to address them."

U.S. General Services Administration
1275 First Street, NE
Washington, DC 20417
Telephone: (202) 501-0800
Fax: (202) 219-1243

2

See comment 2.

GAO limited its review to Facebook, Twitter, and YouTube. As discussed on an April 14 teleconference and through additional information provided Mr. Marinos relative to the draft statement of facts, we would like to clarify here again that GSA uses Facebook, YouTube, and Twitter for one-way marketing. No PII is sought or provided to GSA as a result of our use of Facebook, YouTube, or Twitter. Therefore, a PIA is unnecessary. In contrast, when GSA plans to use social media providers for two-way communication wherein PII is potentially received from the public, GSA does indeed "conduct and document a privacy impact assessment that evaluates potential privacy risks associated with agency use of social media services and identifies protections to address them." Furthermore, GSA publically posts its PIAs as illustrated by these examples:

Challenge Post PIA
http://www.gsa.gov/graphics/staffoffices/ChallengeGovPIA.doc

Citizen Engagement PIA
http://www.gsa.gov/graphics/staffoffices/CEP_Tools_PIA_061810.doc

Open Government Citizen Engagement Tool
http://www.gsa.gov/graphics/staffoffices/OpenGovtEngagementToolOCSC_021610.doc

Technical comments that update and clarify statements in the draft report are enclosed. Should you have any questions, please do not hesitate to contact me. Staff inquiries may be directed to Ms. Casey Coleman, Chief Information Officer. She can be reached at (202) 501-1000.

Sincerely,

Martha Johnson
Administrator

Enclosure

cc: Mr. Gregory C. Wilshusen,
Director, Information Technology Security Issues
GAO

The following are GAO's comments to the General Services
Administration's letter dated June 3, 2011.

## GAO Comments

1. After reviewing additional comments provided by agency
   representatives, we updated our report to indicate that the agency
   asserted that it is taking actions to develop privacy policies addressing
   the agency's use of PII made available through social media services.
   We have not evaluated these actions.

2. We believe that a PIA is required. As indicated in our report, OMB's
   guidance states that when an agency takes action that causes PII to
   become accessible to agency officials—such as posting information on
   a Facebook page that allows the public to comment—PIAs are
   required. Without a PIA, the agency may lack assurance that all
   potential privacy risks have been evaluated and that protections have
   been identified to mitigate them

# Appendix VIII: Comments from the Department of Defense

Note: GAO's comments supplementing those in the report's text appear at the end of this appendix.

Mr. Gregory C. Wilshusen
Director, Information Security Issues
U.S. Government Accountability Office
441 G Street, NW
Washington, DC 20548

Dear Mr. Wilshusen:

See comment 1.

In response to the GAO Draft Report, GAO-11-605, "SOCIAL MEDIA: Federal Agencies Need Policies and Procedures for Managing and Protecting Information They Access and Disseminate," dated May 6, 2011 (GAO Code 311048), the Department of Defense concurs with the first of the two recommendations. A privacy impact assessment that evaluates potential privacy risks associated with agency use of social media services and identifies protections to address those risks has been conducted. Documentation is in the final approval process and is planned for completion by July 29, 2011.

See comment 2.

Regarding the second recommendation, documentation of the assessment of security risks associated with DoD use of social media and identification of security controls that can be used to mitigate the identified risks was provided to your office on May 12, 2011. Consequently, your office has agreed to omit this recommendation from the final report.

The point of contact for this matter is Mr. Terry Davis, at email: terry.w.davis@osd.mil and telephone: 703-699-0107.

Sincerely,

Teresa M. Takai
Principal Deputy

The following are GAO's comments to the Department of Defense's letter dated May 27, 2011.

## GAO Comments

1. We updated our report to indicate that the department asserted that it is taking actions to develop a PIA for its social media use, although it has not yet been finalized. We have not evaluated these actions.

2. After reviewing the additional documentation provided, we agree that the department met the requirement of conducting and documenting a security risk assessment. We modified the report, as appropriate, and removed the recommendation.

# Appendix IX: Comments from the Department of Education

Note: GAO's comments supplementing those in the report's text appear at the end of this appendix.

Mr. Gregory C. Wilshusen
Director, Information Security Issues
U.S. Government Accountability Office
441 G Street, NW
Washington, DC 20548

Dear Mr. Wilshusen:

I am writing in response to the recommendation made in the U.S. Government Accountability Office (GAO) draft report, "Social Media: Federal Agencies Need Policies and Procedures for Managing and Protecting Information They Access and Disseminate" (GAO-11-605). I appreciate the opportunity to comment on the draft report on behalf of the U.S. Department of Education (Department).

Social media tools are important to the Department's efforts to communicate with the public. We are using Facebook, Twitter, You Tube, and a blog to share information and engage the public in a conversation about improving education. (See our list of social media pages and accounts at http://www2.ed.gov/about/overview/focus/social-media.html.) And we are taking steps to ensure that when we use social media, we meet our legal obligations and requirements.

The Department's response to the report's recommendation follows, along with additional comments on Table 2 in the report.

**Recommendation:** *To ensure that appropriate privacy measures are in place when commercially provided social media services are used, we recommend that the Secretary of Education take the following action.*
  * *Update privacy policies to describe whether PII made available through use of social media services is collected and used.*

**Response:** The Department agrees with GAO's recommendation. Our privacy policy has been updated to describe how we treat personally identifiable information (PII). The policy includes the following statement:

See comment 1.

"...please be aware that the privacy protection provided at ED.gov may not be available on [these] third-party sites. Please note that when ED uses social media sites, ED does not collect or in any way use personally identifiable information."

To read our complete privacy policy, please see the materials at the following Web address: http://www2.ed.gov/notices/privacy/index.html#social-media.

400 MARYLAND AVE.. S.W.. WASHINGTON, DC 20202-3500
www.ed.gov

*Our mission is to ensure equal access to education and to promote educational excellence throughout the nation.*

In addition, the Department would like to comment on several points in the draft report.

1. Table 2 in the draft report indicates that the Department has not "document[ed] processes and policies and record-keeping roles and responsibilities for how social media records are identified and managed."

See comment 2.

The Privacy, Information, and Records Management Services team in our Office of Management developed and distributed for comment in early May 2011 draft guidance for records management related to social media. This guidance describes the principles and questions that the Department's principal offices and staff will use when analyzing, scheduling, and managing records related to social media. This guidance is under review within the Department, and we expect it to be issued in final form by the end of fiscal year (FY) 2011.

2. Table 2 indicates that the Department has not "conduct[ed] privacy impact assessment for social media use."

See comment 3.

The Privacy, Information, and Records Management Services team in the Department's Office of Management developed and distributed in early May 2011 a draft "Privacy Impact Assessment for Social Media Websites and Applications." This draft is under review within the Department, and we expect it to be issued in final form by the end of FY 2011.

This draft privacy impact assessment (PIA) covers all Department current and authorized social media Web sites and applications that are functionally comparable, including those owned by the Department or by a third party. None of the social media Web sites and applications covered by the PIA solicit, collect, maintain, or disseminate sensitive PII from individuals who interact with these authorized social media Web sites and applications. For any social media uses that raise privacy risks that are distinct and different from those covered by this PIA, the Department will prepare a separate PIA.

3. Table 2 indicates that the Department has not "identify[ed] security risks associated with agency use of social media and security controls to mitigate risks."

See comment 4.

We have in fact taken steps to identify and contain security risks by significantly limiting social media access and use to only those Department staff who have articulated a business need for such access or use. We have also conducted a security risk assessment of social media. This risk assessment recommends policy, procedural, and technical mitigations that may be employed to lessen the potential impact of these risks. The risk assessment is in draft and has not yet been finalized.

4. Finally, we have developed a draft comprehensive social media policy for the Department that will govern the use of social media for all employees. This policy discusses privacy, security, records management, and related legal requirements. The

development of its contents was coordinated with the development of the above-mentioned records management policy and PIA. This social media policy is currently under review within the Department, and we expect it to be issued in final form by the end of FY 2011.

We appreciate the opportunity to review the draft report and comment on the recommendation. If you have any questions or concerns regarding our response, please have your staff contact Kirk Winters at (202) 401-3540 or kirk.winters@ed.gov.

Sincerely,

5/25/11

Peter Cunningham
Assistant Secretary

The following are GAO's comments to the Department of Education's letter dated May 25, 2011.

## GAO Comments

1. After reviewing the privacy policy on the department's Web site, we updated our report to indicate that the department asserted that it is taking actions to develop privacy policies addressing the agency's use of PII made available through social media services. We confirmed these actions.

2. After reviewing additional efforts stated by the department, we updated our report to indicate that the department asserted that it is taking actions to develop records management guidance for social media use, although such guidance has not yet been finalized. We have not evaluated these actions.

3. After reviewing additional efforts stated by the department, we updated our report to indicate that the department asserted that it is taking actions to conduct and document a PIA related to its use of social media, although it has not yet been finalized. We have not evaluated these actions.

4. After reviewing additional efforts stated by the department, we updated our report to indicate that the department asserted that it is taking actions to conduct and document a security risk assessment related to its use of social media, although the assessment has not yet been finalized. We have not evaluated these actions.

# Appendix X: Comments from the Department of Homeland Security

Note: GAO's comments supplementing those in the report's text appear at the end of this appendix.

June 6, 2011

Gregory C. Wilshusen
Director
Information Security Issues
U.S. Government Accountability Office
441 G Street, NW
Washington, DC 20548

Re:    Draft Report GAO-11-605, "SOCIAL MEDIA:  Federal Agencies Need Policies
       and Procedures for Managing and Protecting Information They Access and
       Disseminate"

Dear Mr. Wilshusen:

Thank you for the opportunity to review and comment on this draft report.  The U.S.
Department of Homeland Security (DHS) appreciates the U.S. Government
Accountability Office's (GAO's) work in planning and conducting its review and issuing
this report.

We are pleased to note the draft report is broadly supportive of the Department's efforts
to develop and implement policies and procedures to address the challenges of managing
and protecting information accessed and disseminated using social media services.  For
example, the report recognizes that DHS has updated its privacy policy to discuss the use
of personally identifiable information made available through these services and to
prohibit the collection of such information by DHS officials.

The draft report also recognizes DHS conducted a privacy impact assessment that
assessed the risks of the Agency's use of social networking tools, including the potential
for Agency access to the personal information of individuals interacting with the
Department on such sites.  Moreover, the one report recommendation directed at DHS,
which we plan to implement, is consistent with the DHS Chief Information Security
Officer's (CISO's) mission of ensuring the security of the Department's systems and
information.  Nonetheless, DHS does not believe the report appropriately recognizes
existing Departmental policy for use of social media services.  For example, DHS'
existing policy and procedures have required risk assessments to be performed prior to
implementing information systems and new technologies such as social media since
January 2003.

To better highlight policy requirements related to the new social media technologies, in
July 2009, DHS established a separate section in the policy dedicated to social media
(Section 3.16 – Social Media, *DHS Sensitive Systems Policy Directive 4300A*).

See comment 1.

In late May 2011, DHS also finalized the *DHS 4300A Sensitive Systems Handbook, Attachment X – Social Media*. Attachment X expands on the existing DHS policy provided in Section 3.16 - *Social Media, DHS Sensitive Systems Policy Directive 4300A,* and DHS Management Directive (MD) 4400.1, *Web (Internet, Intranet, and Extranet Information) and Information Systems.*

Attachment X also provides information security guidance regarding official (work-related) and unofficial (personal) social media use within and outside the Department network. It specifically describes the governance of social media sites across DHS and addresses the use of social media technologies in three scenarios:

- Required Work-Related Use
- Unofficial/Personal Use at Work
- Unofficial/Personal Use Outside of Work

Additionally, Attachment X addresses social media and its associated risks and best practices and guidance regarding social media use by DHS employees and contractors.

The draft report contained one recommendation directed to DHS. Specifically, to ensure that appropriate security measures are in place when commercially-provided social media services are used, GAO recommend that the Secretary of Homeland Security:

**Recommendation:** Conduct and document a security risk assessment to assess security threats associated with agency use of commercially-provided social media services and identify security controls that can be used to mitigate the identified threats.

**Response:** Concur. The DHS CISO will conduct and document the recommended security risk assessment. Estimated completion date: March 1, 2012.

Again, thank you for the opportunity to review and comment on this draft report. We look forward to working with you on future Homeland Security issues.

Sincerely,

Jim H. Crumpacker
Director
Departmental GAO/OIG Liaison Office

2

The following are GAO's comments to the Department of Homeland
Security's letter dated June 6, 2011.

## GAO Comments

1. After reviewing additional efforts stated by the department, we
   updated our report to indicate that the department asserted that it is
   taking actions to conduct and document a security risk assessment
   related to its use of social media, although the assessment has not yet
   been finalized. We have not evaluated these actions.

# Appendix XI: Comments from the Department of Housing and Urban Development

Note: GAO's comments supplementing those in the report's text appear at the end of this appendix.

CHIEF INFORMATION OFFICER

MAY 2 7 2011

Mr. Gregory C. Wilshusen
Director,
Information Technology
U.S. Government Accountability Office
441 G Street, NW
Washington, DC 20548

Dear Mr. Wilshusen:

Thank you for the opportunity to comment on the Government Accountability Office (GAO) draft report entitled, *Social Media: Federal Agencies Need Policies and Procedures for Managing and Protecting Information They Access and Disseminate* (GAO-11-605).

The Department of Housing and Urban Development (HUD) reviewed the draft report and concurs with the following recommendation for executive action:

To ensure that appropriate security measures are in place when commercially provided social media services are used, we recommend that the Secretary of Housing and Urban Development take the following action.

- Conduct and document a security risk assessment to assess security threats associated with agency use of Twitter and YouTube and identify security controls that can be used to mitigate the identified threats.

See comment 1.

HUD complied with the recommendation by conducting security risk assessments on agency use of Twitter and YouTube. The enclosed documentation will verify that appropriate security controls are in place to mitigate identified risks.

If you have any questions or require additional information, please contact Joyce M. Little, Director, Office of Investment Strategies Policy and Management at (202) 402-7404.

Sincerely,

Jerry E. Williams
Chief Information Officer

Enclosures

The following are GAO's comments to the Department of Housing and
Urban Development's letter dated May 27, 2011.

## GAO Comments

1. After reviewing the additional documentation provided, we updated
   our report to indicate that the department asserted that it is taking
   actions to conduct and document a security risk assessment related to
   its use of social media. We confirmed these actions.

# Appendix XII: Comments from the Department of Veterans Affairs

Note: GAO's comments supplementing those in the report's text appear at the end of this appendix.

Mr. Randall B. Williamson
Director, Health Care
U.S. Government Accountability Office
441 G Street, NW
Washington, DC  20548

Dear Mr. Williamson:

The Department of Veterans Affairs (VA) has reviewed the Government Accountability Office's (GAO) draft report, *"SOCIAL MEDIA: Federal Agencies Need Policies and Procedures for Managing and Protecting Information They Access and Disseminate"* (GAO-11-605), and generally agrees with GAO's conclusions and concurs with GAO's recommendations to the Department.

The enclosure specifically addresses GAO's recommendations and provides comments to the report.  VA appreciates the opportunity to comment on your draft report.

Sincerely,

John R. Gingrich
Chief of Staff

Enclosure

Enclosure

**Department of Veterans Affairs (VA) Comments to
Government Accountability Office (GAO) Draft Report**
*SOCIAL MEDIA: Federal Agencies Need Policies and Procedures for Managing
and Protecting Information They Access and Disseminate*
*(GAO-11-605)*

To ensure that appropriate records management and privacy measures are in place
when commercially provided social media services are used, GAO recommends that
the Secretary of Veterans Affairs take the following two actions:

**Recommendation 1:** Add records management guidance to agency social media
policies that describes records management processes and policies and recordkeeping
roles and responsibilities.

See comment 1.

**VA Comment:** Concur. Records management guidance has been added to the draft
Social Media Policy which is currently in concurrence within the Department.

**Recommendation 2:** Conduct and document a privacy impact assessment that
evaluates potential privacy risks associated with agency use of social media services
and identifies protections to address them.

See comment 2.

**Comments:** Concur. VA understands and acknowledges the need for conducting
Privacy Impact Assessments (PIA) on social media services in use by the Department
in order to identify and address privacy risks associated with the use of these services,
and to provide protections that address these risks. The Office of Public and
Intergovernmental Affairs (OPIA) will be working closely with the Office of Information
and Technology and health experts in the Veterans Health Administration to ensure that
the appropriate assessments and protections are conducted and implemented.
OPIA drafted a template for conducting these PIAs. VA estimates the PIA acceptance
will be completed by June 30, 2011.

VA is also in the process of making changes to its draft Web-based Collaboration Tools
policy. The changes will require PIAs for all Web-based collaboration tools that will be
placed on VA's intranet, Internet, or for any social media website hosted by a third party.

1

The following are GAO's comments to the Department of Veterans Affairs'
letter dated May 31, 2011.

## GAO Comments

1. After reviewing additional comments provided by department
representatives, we updated our report to indicate that the department
asserted that it is taking actions to develop records management
guidance for social media use, although the guidance has not yet been
finalized. We have not evaluated these actions.

2. After reviewing additional comments provided by department
representatives, we updated our report to indicate that the department
asserted that it is taking actions to develop a PIA for its social media
use, although the PIA has not yet been finalized. We have not evaluated
these actions.

# Appendix XIII: Comments from the Environmental Protection Agency

Note: GAO's comments supplementing those in the report's text appear at the end of this appendix.

MAY 2 5 2011

OFFICE OF
ENVIRONMENTAL INFORMATION

Mr. Gregory C. Wilshusen
Director
Information Security Issues
U.S. Government Accountability Office
441 G Street, NW
Washington, DC 20548

Re: EPA Comments on the Government Accountability Office's (GAO) draft report entitled *Social Media: Federal Agencies Need Policies and Procedures for Managing and Protecting Information They Access and Disseminate (GAO-11-605)*

Dear Mr. Wilshusen:

This letter provides the U.S. Environmental Protection Agency's (EPA) comments on GAO's draft report entitled *Social Media: Federal Agencies Need Policies and Procedures for Managing and Protecting Information They Access and Disseminate (GAO-11-605)*. EPA appreciates the review GAO has conducted with 24 major agencies, as well as the opportunity to provide comments on this draft report.

EPA understands the importance of access to its environmental information and is fully committed to using social media to make its information available to an even wider audience. This is a timely GAO report as social media offers many exciting opportunities, while at the same time creating special challenges for federal agencies.

Here at EPA, we understand the need to provide our staff with policies, procedures and guidance as they continue to implement social media. With the need to ensure that proper records are maintained, that privacy is protected, and that EPA's information systems are protected from security threats and risks, it is vital that EPA have clear processes in place to address these issues. EPA is currently in the final stages of completing the Social Media Policy along with three accompanying procedures: Using Social Media Internally at EPA, Using Social Media to Communicate with the Public, and Representing EPA Online Using Social Media.

EPA appreciates the recommendations set forth in the GAO draft report. As we continue to move forward with the use of social media, the Agency has made these recommendations a priority.

I have enclosed our specific technical comments to the GAO recommendations. If you would like to discuss these matters further, please contact me at 202-564-6665, or your staff may contact Todd Holderman, Director of the Information Access Division, at 202-564-8598.

Sincerely,

Malcolm D. Jackson
Assistant Administrator
and Chief Information Officer

Enclosure

cc: Seth Oster, OEAEE
    Robin Gonzalez, OIAA
    Andrew Battin, OIC
    Vaughn Noga, OTOP

EPA's Response to GAO Recommendations

ENVIRONMENTAL PROTECTION AGENCY:  Draft GAO Report (GAO-11-605):
Social Media: *Federal Agencies Need Policies and Procedures for Managing and
Protecting Information They Access and Disseminate.*

Lead Office:  Office of Environmental Information

Participating Offices:  Office of Information Analysis and Access, Office of Information
Collection, and the Office of External Affairs and Environmental Education.

GAO Recommendation

Conduct and document a privacy impact assessment that evaluates potential privacy risks
associated with agency use of social media services and identifies protections to address
them.

EPA Response

See comment 1.

> EPA agrees.  The Agency's Office of External Affairs and Environmental
> Education (OEAEE) is responsible for the planning, development and review of
> all Agency web products intended for the public and targeted audiences.  OEAEE
> will conduct a privacy impact assessment (PIA) of EPA's use of social media
> services and identify protections to mitigate any risks identified.  The PIA will be
> completed by June 30, 2011.

GAO Recommendation

Conduct and document a security risk assessment to assess security threats associated
with agency use of commercially provided social media services and identify security
controls that can be used to mitigate the identified threats.

EPA Response

See comment 2.

> EPA agrees.  The Environmental Protection Agency (EPA) will assess risks
> associated with commercially provided social media services we use. Risks will
> be assessed by identifying associated threats and vulnerabilities and evaluating
> them against likelihood of occurrence and adverse impact.  We will identify
> proper security controls that can be used to mitigate identified risks to an
> acceptable level.  The risk assessment will be completed by June 1, 2012.

The following are GAO's comments to the Environmental Protection
Agency's letter dated May 25, 2011.

## GAO Comments

1.  After reviewing additional comments provided by agency
    representatives, we updated our report to indicate that the agency
    asserted that it is taking actions to develop a PIA for its social media
    use, although the PIA has not yet been finalized. We have not evaluated
    these actions.

2.  After reviewing additional comments provided by agency
    representatives, we updated our report to indicate that the agency
    asserted taking actions to develop a security risk assessment for social
    media use, although the assessment has not yet been finalized. We
    have not evaluated these actions.

# Appendix XIV: Comments from the National Aeronautics and Space Administration

Note: GAO's comments supplementing those in the report's text appear at the end of this appendix.

**MAY 3 1 2011**

Reply to Attn of:

Office of the Chief Information Officer

Mr. Gregory C. Wilshusen
Director, Information Security Issues
United States Government Accountability Office
Washington, DC 20548

Dear Mr. Wilshusen:

The National Aeronautics and Space Administration (NASA) appreciates the opportunity to review and comment on your draft report entitled, "Social Media: Federal Agencies Need Policies and Procedures for Managing and Protecting Information They Access and Disseminate" (GAO-11-605). In the draft report, GAO makes three recommendations to ensure that appropriate privacy and security measures are in place when commercially provided social media services are used by NASA, specifically:

**Recommendation 1:** The Administrator of the National Aeronautics and Space Administration update privacy policies to describe whether PII made available through use of social media services is collected and used.

See comment 1.

**Management Response:** NASA concurs with the GAO recommendation. The NASA Chief Information Officer (CIO) has already disseminated guidance regarding privacy implications in the use of social media through a CIO memorandum on "Appropriate Use of Web Technologies," issued August 12, 2010, through an Agency-wide user notification and through the NASA CIO Web site. In addition, NASA has been reviewing all agency privacy policies and will update these policies to address appropriate security measures, prohibitions, and controls required for the use of social media services.

**Recommendation 2:** The Administrator of the National Aeronautics and Space Administration conduct and document a privacy impact assessment that evaluates potential privacy risks associated with agency use of social media services and identifies protections to address them.

See comment 2.

**Management Response:** NASA concurs with the GAO recommendation. NASA policy requires that Information and Privacy Threshold Analyses (IPTAs), and, if appropriate, full Privacy Impact Assessments (PIAs), be conducted on all known systems. However, the data generated or collected by the social media services within the scope of this GAO engagement (Facebook, YouTube, Twitter) exist outside of the NASA enterprise architecture and administrative control. As previously reported to GAO on

2

January 10, 2011, no personally identifiable information is collected from comments
posted by the public on NASA's own Facebook, YouTube, and Twitter pages.
Nevertheless, NASA is currently developing a PIA of these social media services in
accordance with OMB Memorandum 10-23, which requires an adapted PIA whenever an
Agency's use of a third-party Web site or application makes PII available to the Agency.
Using all information available to NASA, this PIA will evaluate potential privacy risks
and identify every possible protection to address these risks.

**Recommendation 3:** The Administrator of the National Aeronautics and Space
Administration conduct and document a security risk assessment to assess security threats
associated with agency use of commercially provided social media services and identify
security controls that can be used to mitigate the identified threats.

See comment 3.

**Management Response:** NASA concurs with the GAO recommendation. NASA is
conducting and documenting a security risk assessment to assess security threats
associated with Agency use of commercially provided social media services, which will
identify or verify common security controls. In addition, NASA periodically reviews the
security posture of commercial social media products for new vulnerabilities and updates
its infrastructure or procedures accordingly. NASA has also added social media risks to
the Agency's risk profile and updated information security training to educate its
community on the risks associated with commercial social media services.

If you have any questions or require additional information, please contact the NASA
Deputy CIO for IT Security, Valarie Burks at (202) 358-3716.

Sincerely,

Linda Cureton
Chief Information Officer

The following are GAO's comments to the National Aeronautics and Space Administration's letter dated May 31, 2011.

## GAO Comments

1. After reviewing additional efforts stated by the agency, we updated our report to indicate that the agency has plans to develop privacy policies addressing the agency's use of PII made available through social media services.

2. After reviewing additional comments provided by agency representatives, we updated our report to indicate that the agency asserted that it is taking actions to develop a PIA for its social media use, although the PIA has not yet been finalized. We have not evaluated these actions.

3. After reviewing additional comments provided by agency representatives, we updated our report to indicate that the agency asserted that it is taking actions to develop a security risk assessment for social media use, although the assessment has not yet been finalized. We have not evaluated these actions.

# Appendix XV: Comments from the Office of Personnel Management

Note: GAO's comments supplementing those in the report's text appear at the end of this appendix.

Chief Information
Officer

May 24, 2011

Mr. Gregory C. Wilshusen, Director
Information Security Issues
U.S. Government Accountability Office
441 G Street, N.W.
Washington, DC 20548

Dear Mr. Wilshusen:

We recognize that even the most well run programs can benefit from an external evaluation and we appreciate the input of the Government Accountability Office as we continue to enhance our social media program. We have reviewed your draft audit report (GAO-11-605) titled Social Media: Federal Agencies Need Policies and Procedures for Managing and Protecting Information and are in concurrence with the two recommendations for Office of Personnel Management (OPM) identified in the report. Specific responses to your recommendations are provided below.

**Response to Recommendations**

RECOMMENDATION: To ensure that appropriate privacy and security measures are in place when commercially provided social media services are used, we recommend that the Director of the OPM take the following two actions:

- Conduct and document a privacy impact assessment that evaluates potential privacy risks associated with agency use of social media services and identifies protections to address them.
- Conduct and document a security risk assessment to assess security threats associated with agency use of commercially provided social media services and identify security controls that can be used to mitigate the identified threats.

See comment 1.

MANAGEMENT RESPONSE: Concur. OPM shall conduct a privacy impact assessment and a security risk assessment as stated in the recommendation. We will complete these assessments no later than September 30, 2011.

Sincerely,

Matthew E. Perry
Chief Information Officer

www.opm.gov          Recruit, Retain and Honor a World-Class Workforce to Serve the American People          www.usajobs.gov

The following are GAO's comments to the Office of Personnel
Management's letter dated May 24, 2011.

## GAO Comments

1. After reviewing additional comments and materials provided by
   agency representatives, we updated our report to indicate that the
   agency asserted that it is taking actions to develop both a PIA and a
   security risk assessment for its social media use. We have not
   evaluated these actions.

# Appendix XVI: Comments from the Social Security Administration

Note: GAO's comments
supplementing those in
the report's text appear at
the end of this appendix.

May 26, 2011

Mr. Gregory Wilshusen
Director, Information Security Issues
United States Government Accountability Office
441 G. Street, NW
Washington, D.C.  20548

Dear Mr. Wilshusen:

Thank you for the opportunity to review your draft report, "Social Media: Federal Agencies
Need Policies and Procedures for Managing and Protecting Information They Access and
Disseminate."  We have enclosed our response to your report.

If you have any questions, please contact me or have your staff contact Chris Molander, Senior
Advisor, Audit Management and Liaison Staff, at (410) 965-7401.

Sincerely.

Dean S. Landis
Deputy Chief of Staff

Enclosure

SOCIAL SECURITY ADMINISTRATION    BALTIMORE. MD 21235-0001

See comment 1.

**SOCIAL SECURITY ADMINISTRATION COMMENTS ON THE GOVERNMENT ACCOUNTABILITY OFFICE DRAFT REPORT, "SOCIAL MEDIA: FEDERAL AGENCIES NEED POLICIES AND PROCEDURES FOR MANAGING AND PROTECTING INFORMATION THEY ACCESS AND DISSEMINATE" (GAO-11-605)**

We offer the following comment.

**Recommendation**

To ensure that appropriate privacy measures are in place when commercially provided social media services are used, we recommend that the Commissioner of the Social Security Administration take the following action.

- Update privacy policies to describe whether PII made available through use of social media services is collected and used.

**Response**

We do not use or collect PII made available through social media services. However, we will update our privacy policy to reflect that fact and post the update to our agency website.

The following are GAO's comments to the Social Security Administration's letter dated May 26, 2011.

## GAO Comments

1. After reviewing additional comments stated by the agency, we updated our report to indicate that the agency has plans to develop privacy policies addressing the agency's use of PII made available through social media services.

# Appendix XVII: Comments from the U.S. Agency for International Development

Note: GAO's comments supplementing those in the report's text appear at the end of this appendix.

Gregory C. Wilshusen
Director, Information Security Issues
U.S. Government Accountability Office
Washington, DC  20548

Dear Mr. Wilshusen,

I am pleased to provide the U.S. Agency for International Development's formal response to the GAO draft report entitled "SOCIAL MEDIA: Federal Agencies Need Policies and Procedures for Managing and Protecting Information They Access and Disseminate" (GAO-11-605).

The enclosed USAID comments are provided for incorporation with this letter as an appendix to the final report.

Thank you for the opportunity to respond to the GAO draft report and for the courtesies extended by your staff in the conduct of this audit review.

Sincerely,

Sean Carroll
Chief Operating Officer
U.S. Agency for International Development

Enclosure: a/s

- 2 -

**USAID COMMENTS ON GAO DRAFT REPORT No. GAO-11-605**

**Recommendation 1:** To ensure that appropriate records management and security measures are in place when commercially provided social media services are used, we recommend that the Administrator of the U.S. Agency for International Development (USAID) take the following action: Add records management guidance to agency social media policies that describes records management processes and policies and recordkeeping roles and responsibilities.

See comment 1.

**Response:** USAID concurs with recommendation 1. USAID recognizes the importance of adding sound records management guidance to the agency's social media policies. The Information and Records Division in the Bureau for Management's Office of Management Services is currently reviewing the various social media activities in which the agency is involved, and will establish records management guidance that will effectively apply lifecycle management and appropriate records disposition authority to the electronic record content published by USAID on social media sites. Target Completion Date: December 31, 2011

**Recommendation 2:** To ensure that appropriate records management and security measures are in place when commercially provided social media services are used, we recommend that the Administrator of the U.S. Agency for International Development take the following action, conduct and document a security risk assessment to assess security threats associated with agency use of commercially provided social media services and identify security controls that can be used to mitigate the identified threats.

See comment 2.

**Response:** The Chief Information Security Officer (CISO) concurs with recommendation 2. CISO will conduct a full risk assessment, identify security controls or compensating controls and/or create a plan of action and milestones where necessary. Target Completion Date: June 3, 2011.

The following are GAO's comments to the U.S. Agency for International Development's letter received on May 27, 2011.

## GAO Comments

1. After reviewing additional comments provided by agency representatives, we updated our report to indicate that the agency asserted that it is taking actions to develop records management guidance for social media use. We have not evaluated these actions.

2. After reviewing additional comments provided by agency representatives, we updated our report to indicate that the agency asserted that it is taking actions to develop a security risk assessment for social media use, although the assessment has not yet been finalized. We have not evaluated these actions.

# Appendix XVIII: GAO Contact and Staff Acknowledgments

| | |
|---|---|
| **GAO Contact** | Gregory C. Wilshusen, (202) 512-6244 or wilshuseng@gao.gov |
| **Staff Acknowledgments** | In addition to the contact above, John de Ferrari, Assistant Director; Sher`rie Bacon; Marisol Cruz; Jennifer Franks; Fatima Jahan; Nicole Jarvis; Nick Marinos; Lee McCracken; Thomas Murphy; Constantine Papanastasiou; David Plocher; Dana Pon; Matthew Strain; and Jeffrey Woodward made key contributions to this report. |